The Body as
Shadow

*"The body is the canvas upon which
the soul paints its miseries."*
Anais Nin

Eleanor Limmer M.S.W.

BALBOA.
PRESS
A DIVISION OF HAY HOUSE

Balboa Press books may be ordered through booksellers or by contacting:

Balboa Press
A Division of Hay House
1663 Liberty Drive
Bloomington, IN 47403
www.balboapress.com
1 (877) 407-4847

Because of the dynamic nature of the Internet, any web addresses or
links contained in this book may have changed since publication and
may no longer be valid. The views expressed in this work are solely those
of the author and do not necessarily reflect the views of the publisher,
and the publisher hereby disclaims any responsibility for them.

The author of this book does not dispense medical advice or prescribe the use
of any technique as a form of treatment for physical, emotional, or medical
problems without the advice of a physician, either directly or indirectly. The
intent of the author is only to offer information of a general nature to help you
in your quest for emotional and spiritual well-being. In the event you use any
of the information in this book for yourself, which is your constitutional right,
the author and the publisher assume no responsibility for your actions.

Any people depicted in stock imagery provided by Thinkstock are models,
and such images are being used for illustrative purposes only.
Certain stock imagery © Thinkstock.

Printed in the United States of America.

ISBN: 978-1-4525-9436-1 (sc)
ISBN: 978-1-4525-9438-5 (hc)
ISBN: 978-1-4525-9437-8 (e)

Library of Congress Control Number: 2014904843

Balboa Press rev. date: 04/09/2014

DEDICATION

To Don, Leah, Eric, Alex, Aden,
Jachary and Maxwell

Acknowledgements

I wish to express my gratitude and appreciation to those whose stories are included in this book. Although their names and other personal information, not related to an illness, have been changed or omitted in respect for privacy and confidentiality, all of the stories included in this book are true. These stories have helped me to better understand the shadow of illness. It was a privilege to share with these individuals the joy and sorrow of their healings.

These stories have been a catalyst to my own healing. I appreciate the strength, vulnerability and courage these people have had to face their dark and light shadows in their efforts to be healthier and wiser. Special thanks go to my husband Don and to my friends for their criticisms and encouragement during my writing process.

Since I am not a physician, I do not prescribe the use of any particular treatment, nor do I give specific medical advice. This book gives general information to enable the reader to make their own choices. I do advocate that they trust their intuitions to guide them and take the time and effort to explore the mental, emotional and physical aspects of their bodily symptoms and illnesses.

Contents

Preface to the Body as Shadow

*T*he shadow is an ally to our true self, and the enemy of our negative ego and idealized false self. While the negative ego lies to us and takes away our strength, the shadow is there to return it to us. The shadow is the receptacle of our potential power. It takes much energy to repress, suppress and reject what comes naturally to us like flight to an eagle. If you have ever watched a caged wild animal pace, you know the feeling of frustration that comes with unhealthy confinement.

The shadow is not just a projection of our darkness, nor of our light, though it does hold that light and darkness, until we are ready to recognize and either use it or release it. Besides holding our darkness, the shadow holds and knows our potential power, the purposes we desired to achieve in this incarnation. A healthy person is powerful. It is the shadow that holds the power of each sick person to have good health.

The collective shadow of a family or a culture may imprison certain natural talents and abilities. The blue collar family for instance may resist and devalue a daughter whose light shadow is a beautiful singing voice. Likewise, a professional family may insist their son, whose strongest desire is to be a musician in an orchestra, become a lawyer.

The shadow side of illness can awaken us to what we have denied, rejected and abandoned within us that needs to be faced and healed. Traditionally the symptoms of illness are the primary focus of attention. The holistic approach to illness that this book advocates uses these symptoms as signals of what our shadows both light and dark direct us to recognize, own, forgive and change in us.

Chapter One

The Alchemy of Illnesses

*I*t is not an option whether of not we deal with our shadows. If we don't deal with our shadows, in time our shadows will deal with us. If we ignore and reject exploring and doing shadow work, both dark and light, in time the shadow will deal with us in some way; one way this can happen is through illness and physical pain. This is not a punishment from forces outside ourselves, but another way of making us more conscious and responsible for the purposes we committed ourselves to in this life and before our birth.

As part of our souls, our shadows, with their higher consciousness, know us intimately. Just as dreams dramatically address the issues of the dreamer, so do physical ailments accurately symbolize the conflicts of an individual. The shadow *holds* our patterns of greed, envy, control, manipulation, and self-abandonment until we are strong enough to release and transform them, but the shadow itself is not dark and evil.

Kate Duff came to think of healing from her illness as an alchemical process in which it was crucial she be vulnerable to the most inferior or debased places of herself. When she developed chronic fatigue and immune dysfunction syndrome (CFIDS) in 1988, she soon became aware that she was experiencing a profound transformation in which she would never again be her "old self." She describes this transformation in her book *An Alchemy of Illness.* CFIDS is an illness that seemed to her like a bad flu that never went away. As the only remedy for this illness is prolonged rest, Kate for the next two years spent much of her time in bed. During this time she had much time to reflect upon the meaning of her illness. At one point, Kate fell into a deep despair which was accompanied by clear and revealing dreams.

An important step in the process of alchemy is that of resolving the opposites by facing the dark shadow to find the light that is beneath it. One of Kate's dreams encouraged her to make a place for a pack of black dogs-her shadow issues of despair, greed, envy, and hate-at the end of her bed. In another dream, she was told she needed to use her greed as gas to fuel her car. The shadow issue of her greed was difficult for her to face because greed was a quality she detested in others.

Eventually Kate recognized the part of herself that was greedy for books, money, and food. She realized that since it was greed she had to put in her tank, under this greed must be a luminous light energy or intent, her curiosity, or strong desire for understanding, was the opposite of the darkness of greed. It was this light of curiosity and strong desire that cracked the shell of her despair and helped heal her illness. Kate was healed not only of her illness but in the process became a more self-realized individual.

Physical symptoms and illnesses are challenges made visible for us through the symbolism of our bodies. Our bodies are both responsive and resilient in reaction to our thoughts and their related emotions. If we hold the belief in a division between the mental, emotional and physical, we are misunderstanding the relationship of human consciousness to illness. The traditional belief that disease is only physical does not allow us to have a true perspective of our reality and hides from us the shadow conflicts and problems these symptoms can reveal. The error of the limited perspective of a purely physical approach to illness lies

2

in its deficient understanding of the spirituality of the body, and the physical reality of our thoughts and beliefs.

Through my work as a holistic counselor and guided imagery and music therapist, I have had direct experience of the dynamic power consciousness has to heal the physical body from all kinds of illnesses. I have learned that the energy of healing can be directed by our thoughts and images to heal any kind of illness and at the same time dismantle the core shadow beliefs that foster it. To work with our shadow selves in a successful way, we need to listen to the whispers from our bodies so they do not have to come to us in the shouts of a life threatening, debilitating illness. Before a major illness such as cancer or heart disease happens, we have had many more subtle warnings and messages from our bodies. These whispers tell us to *wake up* and *forgive* ourselves, and *to accept* and change aspects of ourselves so we can grow and become more of who we were meant to be.

We are not the victims of our illnesses, and we do have the power to heal ourselves. Illnesses are challenges and warning signals, much like those on the dashboard of a car, messages that tell us we have made an unfortunate detour. They are wake-up calls telling us to pay attention, to be in the moment, so we can become aware of a problem we need to heal. If we ignore these messages, they become more extreme and life threatening. When we resist other gentler warnings, growth can not occur. Our physical bodies challenge us to learn the lessons we have agreed to face in our lives.

By denying those aspects of ourselves such as illness and pretending we have no power to heal ourselves, we also miss the opportunity to consciously and actively heal ourselves. If we view illness as something that just happens to us over which we have no influence, we are stuck in the same unhealthy patterns. Illness can be faced in responsible healing ways that allows us to change our reactions to the factors that lead, for instance, to such things as a dysfunctional immune system. The failure to take an active responsible role in our own life may lead to heart attacks and early death.

Mismanaged anger, for instance, can have a long-term, negative effect on health. Chronic anger problems compromise the immune system. Researchers have found connections between anger and physical illnesses, such as strokes, coronary heart disease, gastric and respiratory conditions. They have also found that high stress levels are a risk factor in developing diabetes and even cancer. Anger is a major mortality risk, especially for women. In one long-term study, women who often suppressed their anger had three times the mortality rate than those who did not. A 2000 study reported in Circulation Magazine found that men and women with even normal blood pressure who were chronically angry were two times as likely to develop coronary heart disease and three times as likely to have a heart attack compared to the least angry subjects.

Carl Jung defined the shadow as the sum of all those rejected vital aspects of reality which people either cannot or will not make conscious and which therefore are placed within their shadow-unconscious. Jung recognized that the body reflected shadow issues people deny, reject and do not like to admit when he wrote, "The body is very often the personification of this shadow of the ego. Sometimes it forms the skeleton in the cupboard, and everybody naturally wants to get rid of such a thing."

Our language is filled with symbolic, metaphoric expressions that give us messages and clues as to the real meaning beneath an illness, such as "stiff-necked" or "tight fisted.' By listening to our bodies, we can become more conscious and aware of the shadow messages they hold for us. The body follows where the mind takes it. Physical symptoms indicate in an honest direct way, what is held for us in our shadows; things that require our awareness in order to heal ourselves. The English language is full of double-entendre meanings and clichés that have direct clues to the meaning of a physical symptom. Expressions such as, "He is thick-skinned," or "Her heart was not in it," give us clues as to how certain symptoms represent psychological attitudes.

The shadow can be unhealthy and dangerous to individuals and society when it remains an unhealed part of our subconscious or unconscious minds. The shadow holds for us emotional patterns involving fear, anger, hurt, and rage that can make us ill. Awareness of these patterns is the first step in healing. An encounter with and dialogue with our shadows can alert us to destructive patterns so we can consciously choose to let them go and replace them with more constructive ones.

To understand the shadow it is necessary to understand the principle of opposite forces that is present both within our psyches and bodies. A physical symptom like the symbol in a dream can compensate for what is missing in the consciousness of the dreamer by complementing, opposing, modifying, confirming or exaggerating the dreamer's conscious attitude. When an individual refuses to become conscious and process the warning signals of their intuitions, dreams or feelings, then the principle of complementary forces can come into effect. When we reject or refuse to accept vital energies such as sexuality or assertiveness on a conscious level, these energies eventually may be expressed in a physical symptom.

It is always wise to stand on the side of the shadow and let the light within it emerge. Since body and mind are holistically intertwined an emotional psychic imbalance will be reflected in a complementary way upon the physical body. If we refuse to recognize and process hurt feelings concerning a particular situation, this hurt eventually can descend into our backs, shoulders and/or hearts.

Eleanor Limmer M.S.W.

HEALING BY CHANGING
FUNDAMENTAL SHADOW BELIEFS

I am a clinical social worker at the Spokane Healing Arts Center. I specialize in helping people heal by discovering the negative ego patterns beneath illnesses. As a holistic counselor for the last thirty years, I have found there are direct ways of healing that address the shadow issues that our bodies express. These shadow patterns reflect what is missing, inhibited or extreme such as too much anger, rage, hurt or despair.

I have learned to trust the feedback system of the body, its body language, or voice alerts us to toxic poisonous patterns, beliefs and feelings within our subconscious, unconscious or emotional-mental bodies. Consciousness forms matter and not the other way around. Our physical ailments are symbolic of our inner beliefs, thoughts and feelings. If we understand the symbolic nature of illness, we do not need to feel controlled by it and can recognize our part in its creation and then can begin the process of taking responsibility for doing whatever we can to heal ourselves and others.

Roger asked for counseling help after being given a diagnosis of terminal cancer of the throat. While exploring with him what his diagnosis meant to him in a symbolic way, Roger told me he was a college professor who had hoped to get tenure when he was inspired by a new idea that he shared with his superior colleague. To his great dismay his superior had betrayed him by publishing his idea without giving him credit for it. Roger was enraged by this betrayal and felt helpless to do, or say anything about this betrayal. He had repressed his angry response and now was suffering from throat cancer.

The relationship between Roger's throat cancer and his repressed rage was apparent, but not something he was able to immediately accept. The messages of illness have more impact and are more readily accepted if we intuitively experience their truth. Roger was a man who depended almost entirely upon his reason and so it was important for him to arrive at his own awareness of the meaning of his symptoms.

The difficulty with a limited perspective that does not allow for an intuitive experience is what is wrong with any exclusively, scientific approach to reality. Whatever experiences do not fit into the hypothesis of this objective, physical approach are merely denied and fall into the cultural shadow created by them. Intuitive knowledge is simply denied. The truth that would heal Roger had to begin with the recognition that the cancer in his throat was not just a random, physical event that attacked him from within or outside. Roger's rage and repressed anger created an environment conducive to cancer.

His illness was an opportunity for him to express and release this anger in an honest and appropriate way. Since he created the stressful environment conducive to cancer, he also could forgive himself and his superior, and do what he could to resolve this unfortunate situation. He could use self-hypnosis to replace his mistaken beliefs about his powerlessness with healthier ones, thus changing his enraged state to a healthier one.

Our shadow souls are more concerned with our mental, emotional and spiritual growth than they are with our physical bodies. Our shadows are neither evil nor negative. They value our lasting spiritual and emotional growth more than the temporary well being of our physical bodies. For this reason it is always important when we are doing work with our shadows through written dialogue or meditation that we ask our higher selves or inner guides to interpret their messages to us. The perspective of the shadow is beyond time and space and its focus is upon our spiritual growth. Our higher selves take into consideration more of our physical needs and human perspectives.

LISTENING TO THE SHADOW
MESSAGES OF THE BODY

If we seek and find the meaning of illnesses, we can give them a healing significance. We do not consciously cause an illness, but we are ultimately responsible for the emotional-mental environment that can foster it. A cancer or other life threatening illness can mean many things related to the life-style of an individual. A cancer may indicate the presence of a chronic pattern of anxiety with its related feelings of anger or fear. The presence of a cancer may indicate a long standing resentment about the past and despair about healing old wounds.

It is possible for an individual to come to an inner knowing of the unique messages an illness carries. We take back our power from illness when we become aware of these messages, and through them we begin to understand and heal destructive patterns of belief and feelings. Patterns of fear, anger, despair, isolation and hopelessness can be recognized as destructive, and life threatening, because they create an environment fostering and engendering illness.

People who experience chronic stress need to look to their psychological environment as one of the main sources of their physical maladies. Most people do not recognize the consequences of chronic stress. The most dangerous consequences of chronic stress are cardiovascular disease, digestive disorders, immune suppression, impaired insulin regulation, and a damaged hippocampus with cognitive and emotional impairment.

The goal of healing ourselves is to respond in a compassionate, empathetic way to our bodies by taking the time to listen to them. We can respond by seeing them as warning signals to alert us to imbalances in need of our attention. Since most of the threats to our body are psychological in nature, it does not help to ignore or deny these threats exist. Nor does it help to make our bodies our adversaries. We have to begin to nurture our bodies, by not only listening to their messages, but by confronting and resolving the source of our chronic stress and struggle.

THE DANGER OF SUPPRESSED OR REPRESSED EMOTIONS

A negative emotion is any emotion that is suppressed, repressed or not expressed honestly and appropriately. To suppress an emotion is to be consciously aware of it, and be unwilling to express it. To repress an emotion is to be so defended against it that the experience is denied. The most destructive emotions, if unresolved, are anger, shame, hurt and fear. When these emotions are expressed well, they are not dangerous, but stuffed in the body they can be a source of illness. Even love can be a negative emotion if it is not properly expressed. Depression and guilt are emotional states that hide anger. Depression is often an expression of anger we feel will get us in trouble. Guilt is anger we think we have no right to have. To heal both guilt and depression, it is necessary to express the anger beneath them honestly and appropriately.

In repression, resentment is shoved beneath our awareness and ignored. Initially, there must be the recognition that resentment is a destructive thing like a weed that pollutes our life energy. This resentment can be imaginatively processed by plucking it out, like we would pull out weeds by the roots, and replacing them with more constructive thoughts.

When we believe that the expression of our emotions is "weak" or unacceptable," we will repress them. We may have learned by the example of "stoical" parents that suppressing feelings is somehow noble. Perhaps we did not learn how to express our emotions honestly and appropriately. Both men and women sometimes believe that expressing hurt or anger honestly is not acceptable. Anger is positive when it activates us to leave situations of oppression.

There are negative consequences to repressing feelings. Unexpressed feelings do not go away, and eventually can affect our bodies through the shadow of a major illness. Anger can be expressed in cancer, and hurt can be expressed in back or neck problems. There are numerous appropriate ways that emotions such as anger can be expressed and released. Anger can be expressed to a friend or counselor, written out in anger letters (that are not sent) and ritually burnt. Anger can also be expressed honestly and appropriately through screaming, hitting pillows or stomping feet.

The expression of feelings is not always enough to resolve them, because some people have hidden agendas or payoff such as self-pity they wish to continue. Dolores, a client who had breast cancer, was angry at one person after another who did not listen to her well enough. We determined the issue was her inner child's unresolved need for attention and love. Dolores was the eleventh child in a large family in which she felt emotionally neglected. She got attention by showing anger. Sometime in her childhood, she had made the fundamental belief that was placed in the forbidden zone of the subconscious where such beliefs are stored: "Without anger I am invisible. If I am not angry people will not see me. I will be weak. No one will take me seriously. I will have no impact."

Anger was her root emotion, and in the process had become a destructive poison to her. This pattern left her lonely, isolated and with a low functioning immune system that probably had triggered her breast cancer. To make her anger her ally, Dolores went into her subconscious to find, destroy and replace this fundamental belief with one that allowed her to have mastery over her anger: "When I have mastery over my anger, people take me more seriously." She also dialogued with a personification of her anger within her subconscious to ask it to become her ally to alert her to what needed her attention. Instead of exploding, she was able to see what she needed to focus upon and why, as a result, she desired to communicate more clearly and effectively. Dolores made peace with her anger, not by fearing or eliminating it, but by facing it and making it, not her friend but her ally.

EXPLORING HOW OUR BODIES REFLECT OUR SHADOWS

To explore where these feelings are stored, we can close our eyes, take three deep breathes, and focus inward. When I began exploring my shadow issues, I became aware of congestion in my throat that made it difficult for me to speak, and it was there because of fears of abandonment and rejection. When I was an adolescent I was shy and developed cysts at my throat. Later in middle-age I had a hypothyroidism with a goiter at my throat. In my white shadow was a strong desire to write and to express myself verbally, to speak up for myself and others. The shadow held my power until I was ready to express it.

Our shadows are not evil; they merely hold our negativity until we are strong enough to face it and let it go. This negativity does not go away because we deny it. The way we can effectively deal with the darkness of the shadow is to face it by *feeling* its impact upon us and others, own it, forgiving ourselves, and then releasing it by choosing to change. Our shadows, as aspects of our souls, are born with us, and therefore they have a consciousness which knows intimately our darkness and light, our strengths and weaknesses.

The shadow is an ally of our true spiritual selves; holding the depth of our spirituality. Our negative egos are the allies of our idealized false selves which urges us to pattern ourselves after what is acceptable to others and society. Our shadows, on the other hand, urge us to be our true, authentic selves. Therefore our shadows are the natural enemy of our negative egos. Our negative egos always lie to us; our shadows and our bodies as reflections of what the shadow holds for us always tell us the truth.

Most holistic health practitioners accept that one of the principal sources of illness are denied emotions, such as anger or fear, that are not expressed and released in a healthy way. Our shadows encourage us to be honest and to face the ugliness of our negativity, but our negative egos resist this honesty. Instead our negative egos encourage us to distract, deny, or discount those aspects of ourselves that we see as ugly and unkind, such as our coldness, anger, self-punishment, martyrdom, control, greed, judgements, self-pity, selfishness or arrogance. One of the ways the shadow returns to us what is denied or hidden is through bodily symptoms and illness. The body openly expresses what we consciously deny, such as our anger, anxiety, our sadness, or our depression.

The shadow speaks to us in symbols and images. There is no more forceful image of our emotional-mental spiritual pain than illness or physical pain. If we have ignored our denied inner pain, or constricted emotions, this pain comes at us through our bodies to get our attention. This mode of communication usually comes when we resist less intrusive ones which come to us through our dreams, inner guidance and relationships.

When we deny or delay the responsibility of expressing our emotions in appropriate ways, there is always the risk that in time these feelings will manifest in illness. Illness then becomes a message expressed in the symbolic form of our bodies. A heart disease often symbolises our inability to express our love or our suppressed hostility. Arthritis in our joints may represent our inability to express our anger or to flow with the changes around us.

Shadow work is inherent in any form of healing because holistic healing always involves being conscious and taking responsibility at last, for feelings and their related thoughts. Denied or hidden thoughts and feelings do not go away. They can be stuffed in a knee joint, a stomach or a heart. In time, these denied emotions will present us with the issues we have not faced, often in the form of illness. We have created the symbols of for instance "cold hands and feet" and can change them.

Michael, a recently retired postal clerk had for years been shrinking physically and emotionally. He feared he would make mistakes and lose the approval of his supervisors. When retirement arrived, it became more and more necessary to face the fundamental beliefs he had concerning his life and old age script. Michael was literally shrinking from Reynaud's Disease. In this disease, the circulation of blood to the hands and feet is poor, symbolizing his having "cold feet" in acting with integrity and spontaneity in the world, lest he make a mistake and not have the approval of others.

Michael had inhibited his natural tendencies to step forward when he was a child, because he feared that he would make mistakes, and not get approval from his parents. He chose early on to become 'the good child.' To heal his fundamental beliefs concerning his need to be "good" if he was to be loved, I asked Michael to go, in meditation, to his subconscious, and ask the person in charge to take him to the forbidden zone where his beliefs were hidden. Michael saw his subconscious as a library with many rooms and books.

In meditation, he allowed the head librarian to show him the script, or book, containing his beliefs, "I do not deserve love because I am not perfect or good enough." As a result of this belief, John could see that his focus had been on earning the approval of unavailable women as well as authority figures. He asked this head librarian to replace the debilitating beliefs with,

"It is safe to reach and step out to love and be loved," and "I deserve love, and I am good enough, and loving enough to love and be loved."

Michael needed to remind himself frequently that his "cold feet and hands" were symbolic and not a permanent condition. To reinforce these new beliefs he displayed them around his home in all the common places he looked, such as on the refrigerator, the bathroom mirror, the steering wheel of his car, the garage door so that this new belief would be firmly entrenched in his subconscious mind. I then suggested to Michael, he rewrite his old age script in a way that would counteract the entropy of his body. By changing his fundamental beliefs concerning aging, John began to allow himself to be more spontaneous and courageous in his activities and relationships. Consequently, his hands and feet began to heal.

The shadow is a face of the soul which loves us. It nurtures, comforts and works with us. The shadow years begin in early adolescence after our adolescent wounding and last until our mid-fifties. During these years, we are drawn into the dark wound of ourselves. In this, the soul is there to comfort, nurture and heal us from our adolescent wound which can cut us away from the parental and societal version of what we should be. In the shadow years, we are called upon to invent our own identities. The shadow gives us a dark place in which we can retreat to regenerate from our experiments in the world. It is during these middle, shadow years, we have our mid-life crises.

Our souls act in harsh ways during times of discord, disease or tragedy because other avenues of communication have been cut off by us. During these dark times, we can meet our souls and begin to recognize their love and messages to us. We can awaken to a more hopeful, happier way of living. We often deny the presence of our souls because our culture and families have taught us to ignore or discount its vital, dynamic presence.

The face of the shadow-soul is a living, breathing spiritual force. One of the ways you can work with it is to ask it to appear to you in your meditations or dreams. It is important to pay attention to the form it appears in, to learn why it comes as a man or a woman, what its appearance, such as dress tells us, and what is its general message. The shadow is a loving presence which prefers to come in ways other than discord, illness or tragedy. If we give it a voice and allow it to speak to us in our meditations, dreams, and creative expressions, it does not need to find harsher ways to communicate.

HEALING THE BELIEFS AND EMOTIONAL PATTERNS AT THE ROOT OF ILLNESS

The body is the form created by the structure of our fundamental beliefs, choices, and feelings. An illness is a symbolic signal or message of some mental, emotional and spiritual distress we have previously denied and thus finds physical expression in our bodies. A trauma, unhealed at the time it occurs, alters the energy patterns around the body of the one traumatized. These energy patterns are stressful and can lead to illnesses or relationship conflicts. When these stressful patterns occur, they can trigger illnesses such as diabetes or multiple sclerosis that could be prevented or healed.

To heal the pattern beneath an illness it is often necessary to uncover an incident or incidents that are its core issue. These incidents with their related negative beliefs and feelings are negative ego patterns. The human body is a hologram. In a hologram, each part contains the energy of the whole. Our reality also functions as a hologram. The pattern of repressed rage can manifest in many different forms, some of these are back pain, dizziness, headaches, fibromyalgia, or sciatica.

Negative ego patterns are created when the negative emotions accompanying traumas are not healed. These patterns can be considered inner stresses because they activate fear, anger, grief or despair. If we are able to heal the pain and emotions accompanying a trauma when it is happening or shortly thereafter, a pattern is not created in our energetic bodies. These patterns predispose us to be attracted to certain people and kinds of relationships. These relationships have the same theme with different actors or forms. When these energetic patterns are triggered, they can manifest themselves as severe emotional stress or disease.

Negative ego patterns of too much or too little energy disrupt the flow of chi or energy through our chakras to our nervous systems. These patterns are seen by psychics as dark or murky places in our energy fields that can be cleared energetically. To prevent their return, our fundamental beliefs, and their related feeling must change.

These negative patterns of belief and feeling are the remnants from traumatic events we were not able to deal with in the moment, or that occurred during our childhood when we were particularly vulnerable to experiences of shame, abandonment, past life traumas, or physical and emotional abuse. To heal an unhealthy pattern, another healthier one needs to replace it, or the old pattern will in time creep back into the vacuum left. Constrictive emotional patterns involving hate or violence attract experiences of a similar nature such as road rage, accidents or assaults.

Recognizing Chakra Issues as Clues to the Source of Illness

Physical pain is sourced in emotional pain in this life time or in another which we continue to deny, ignore or fail to heal. To bring about real healing rather than merely treating symptoms it is essential to listen to the body. The key is to allow the body to give you a clue as to what a symptom symbolizes. The body like the unconscious speaks in symbols. Its language is the symbolic language of illness. To heal, you have to listen to what this particular pain or illness is telling you.

We are carefully designed creatures. Everything about our body-minds has intelligence, logic and purpose. There is a natural logic and organization within the body's chakra system that indicates the nature of the issues involved. Issues of safety and security will affect the first chakra areas of our body such as the anus buttocks, feet and hands. Psychics and Native Shamans tell us we have a subtle energy or aura body which is close to the physical, penetrating and surrounding the body. This aura is described as being bright and glittery, and changes shape and color with every thought and emotion. The etheric body is sensitive to distortions of thought and feeling held for any length of time; these distortions can eventually harm the physical body.

Our bodies do not generate an aura. The etheric realms generate the energy of our bodies. Our bodies are an expression of our unconscious self. When we use our unconscious minds as garbage bins for all the negative things we don't like we create an interference pattern of fear, hurt or anger that constricts the flow of energy into and around our bodies. Medical intuitives can sense areas of the body where there are "hot spots" or areas in the energy field around an individual that are abnormal. They have either too much or too little energy. Our stresses are located in the area of the body that correspond to the type of stress we are experiencing.

When a fear or anger becomes the motivating force or obsession, we are driven or controlled by it. A loss of emotional or psychological control then creates an internal conflict that allows disease to develop. Every stress is site specific. A fear of failure relates to issues of power so will affect organs in the abdominal area. The chakra area involved in the symptom and the function of this body part are clues to its meaning.

The body, as a reflection of our shadow, holds the issue we can face and heal to become more whole and healthy. The main issue of the chakra area will give us a clue as to what conflicts are involved in an illness:

(1) **First chakra** is known as the source of Kundalini and is called the root chakra because it is the foundation of the physical body and helps us to stay grounded to the earth; it deals with problems involving the anus, hands, feet, sexual organs and issues of security and safety.

(2) **Second chakra** is known as the Sacral chakra and is the foundation of the emotional body. It influences our sexuality and sensuality, sexual organs, reproduction and fertility, and problems involving the wrists, shins and genital areas. It also reflects how open-minded we are and how we relate to others, and to receiving and giving pleasure.

(3) **Third chakra** known as the Solar Plexus represent the mental body, personal power and self-control and is related to problems involving the abdominal area and upper arms and legs, the adrenals, pancreas, liver, gall bladder, kidneys, metabolism and the nervous system, particularly issues involving power struggles/and control.

(4) **Fourth chakra** is the Heart Chakra, which deals with problems involving the heart, lungs, elbows and knees and conflicts concerning self love and love for others,. The thymus is the gland that is related to this chakra.

(5) **Fifth chakra** is known as the Throat chakra; it involves conflicts concerning communication and deals with problems with the thyroid gland, the shoulders, and the throat area.

(6) **Sixth chakra** is known as the Third Eye Chakra and is concerned with problems in the forehead, pituitary, face, eyes, ears, nose, brain and the central nervous system and with intuition, and physic abilities.

(7) **Seventh chakra** is known as the Crown Chakra and deals with problems involving the top of the head, the pineal gland, the central nervous system, the bones and conflicts concerning spiritual issues.

Every negative ego pattern is linked to a chakra through which it releases its information into the central nervous system. When a negative pattern is activated, its toxic energy spills into a chakra compromising the immune response and blocking or stopping the flow of healthy energies. The dark shadow pattern can be considered the source or blueprint of illness, the chakra is the pipeline, the nervous system is the distribution network. Each chakra maps the emotional and physical landscape of our lives. The first chakra is the map related to all the issues of survival and safety. When a dark shadow pattern is triggered concerning safety or survival, dark energies such as fear or anger and its related nuerochemicals clog and prevent this chakra from functioning well.

Chakra Energy Issues and Centers of the Body

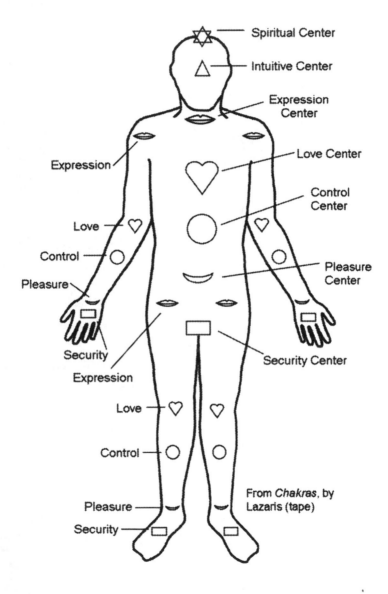

Figure 1

Our chakras have integrity in the sense that they respond in conscious and spontaneous ways. There are no "bad" energies, only heavy or light ones. Judgments, fear, hurt, grief, and shame are heavy energies that clog or obstruct chakras. Each chakra center affects the others and is coordinated like a CD system that has major categories, but minor themes. Each chakra responds in the intensity of the moment in an open and humble way if they are not corroded or damaged.

Chakras never shut down or close completely, but they can be frozen, damaged or rendered ineffective by certain experiences and mind sets. These are as follows:

(1) They can freeze or lock up by either too much emotion such as shame, fear, anger or trauma, or by too little emotion. Too little emotion can come when there is a refusal to feel anger, rage or fear. This frozen condition can also occur when there is too much pain from love and heart-broken experiences, such as that which occurs when someone decides to deny love of self, or love of others.

(2) Chakras can malfunction when there is too much pain, shame, despair, sorrow or loss.

(3) Chakras are blocked or rendered ineffective when there are certain mind sets such as guilt and value-judgment that blind them or make them stagnant.

Most people accept a mechanistic view of the body which medical institutions predominately advocate. In this paradigm, the individual has little power to heal themselves or others, except through physical means such as proper diet, exercise or a dependence upon various physical procedures such as surgery or drugs. The sick individual is then dependent upon their genes, and the entropy that is assumed to follow the aging process. This paradigm rejects psychological holistic approaches that recognize the direct effect of thoughts and emotions upon the body.

EMOTIONS AND NEGATIVE EGO PATTERNS

Candace Pert, a holistic scientist, expressed the relationship of the mind to the body as, "The body is the unconscious mind." The basic design of each of our bodies is formed by conscious beliefs and feelings we choose, and these beliefs and feelings are then acted upon by the unconscious intelligent systems within our bodies. When integrated into the personality, Jung called the affects of the shadow, "ninety percent pure gold." The shadow is what the alchemist of the psyche has to face and resolve to become whole and fulfilled. Within the shadow are the vital energies that can help us be more fulfilled, creative and spiritual. From a larger, spiritual perspective, the shadow is a being within the unconscious, but it is not the unconscious, nor is its force limited to one gender. Although our shadows do hold our dark negativity, they are not that negativity.

In her book *Molecules of Emotion,* the scientist Dr. Pert, emphasizes what is most destructive to the body is not so called negative emotions such as anger or fear, but the bottling up of these emotions, so they become stagnant and are not resolved through expression. Dr. Pert, the former Director of Biological Research at the National Institute of Health, describes the emotional limbic center of the brain, particularly the hypothalamus, as the control center between body and mind, going back and forth between the two, influencing both. In this informational network, the mind and its related emotions communicate and coordinate with all the major systems of the body-the immune, endocrine, nervous and circulatory systems.

Pert describes every cell of the body as a radar receiver that gives and receives messages. There are special messenger cells called neuropeptides that are located throughout the body.

These messengers and their receptor sites are found not only in the brain, but in every system of the body including the immune, endocrine, nervous, and circulatory system. These neuropeptides are described by Pert as, 'the biochemical correlates of emotion." In this function, neuropeptides act as links between the physical, mental, emotional and spiritual. These neuropeptides are like radar discs that send out information from the brain that the cells of our bodies then react to spontaneously. This informational network allows organs from different systems; the heart from the circulatory system and the liver from the digestive system, to influence and affect one another. Messages coming from one location in your body can reach organs and cells in virtually any other part of the body, like a cell phone that works from wherever you happen to be.

The existence of this communication network explains how thoughts and feeling can affect virtually every bodily organ. These thoughts and feelings can have a negative or positive effect. A fight with your spouse, may increase your abdominal cramping and diarrhea, whereas feelings of hope, joy, love and gratitude reduce abdominal pain. This system works in reverse as well; physical pain affects your moods and behavior.

Pert noticed that those places upon the body with the most receptor sites, such as the solar plexus correspond to the major chakra areas of the body. These involve subtle energies that affect the seven major endocrine glands. Chakras can be seen as spheres or disks spinning in all directions. Chakras are the doorways in which divine energy enters our bodies. These energies can be blocked by certain thoughts and emotions.

Negative ego patterns can be located by asking what part of the body holds or feels emotions such as shame, grief, pain, when a traumatic experience is recalled. The term "emotion" as Pert uses it refers to its broadest meaning which includes not only commonly considered contracting emotions such as anger, fear and grief, but also joy, contentment, pleasure, peace, love, achievement, creativity, and safety. Emotions are both thoughts and their related feelings. We cannot think without feeling, or feel without thinking.

Neuropeptides are present when there are certain emotional states such as happiness, depression, fear, grief, or despair. Low levels of serotonin and/or dopamine individually or in combination are thought to be the basis of depression. High levels of norepinephrine and adrenaline are involved in the fear response, anxiety disorders, and panic attacks. When there is long term or chronic stress it is correlated to heart disease, high blood pressure, stroke and many other illnesses.

Since emotional expression is tied to a specific flow of peptides in the body, a chronic suppression of emotions and drives disturbs the flow of this informational network. Emotions that are denied, repressed or not resolved create blockages to both the chakra areas and the related endocrine peptides. Emotions that are expressed honestly and appropriately flow through the energy systems and leave no energy blockages.

DECIPHERING THE SYMBOLIC MESSAGES OF ILLNESS

There is a clear method of accessing the messages of an illness. When we access these messages ourselves they impact us much more deeply and therefore have more potential to heal us. The process of decoding the messages of an illness begins with focusing upon the specific physical symptoms and then asking. "What functions of the body are involved?" Then ask, "What do these symptoms symbolize, or are a metaphor of, in my mental, emotional and spiritual life?" Could you express this in a cliché of the body? (I can't stomach this.) or (I have no voice in the matter.)

Then notice what chakra or energy center is involved and what its main issues are. A chakra is a wheel or vortex of energy that can be seen as a disc or sphere spinning in and out at the same time. These chakras are doorways in which energy enters or leaves the body. (If it is the heart for instance, how are the issues of love involved, including self-love?) "What is the message of your body concerning an inner conflict or problem?"

The person who has symptoms of angina can examine how they give and receive love. Are they always giving, but not receiving love from others? What are their core beliefs about issues of love? Do they fear they will be hurt if they are vulnerable enough to love? What do they believe about the price of love? Do they believe that unless they are struggling or striving they will not deserve love? Bodily symptoms symbolize what is believed and reveal both the dark and light shadow.

I have found many women who suffer from hypothyroidism have a silent rage from the belief and feeling their words or expressions, especially angry ones, have little impact or power on significant others. To decipher the message of a hypothyroidism, it is necessary to begin with the issue of the throat area which is expression. Then ask, "What needs to be expressed, and how can I expressed this honestly and appropriately?" The common treatment for hyperthyroid is a radioactive substance that kills the thyroid. This causes hypothyroidism and a dependency on drugs to replace thyroid for the rest of your life. Killing the messenger by only eliminating the symptom or the organ does not help in the long run, as this message may return in time in another form.

Shadow Work for Chapter One—
The Alchemy of Illness

1. What common patterns of thought and feeling block your health, energy and growth? What needs do you have that are not yet met?

2. How are your illnesses symbolic of your negative ego's patterns?

3. While meditating, scan your body to listen to those areas where there is pain and tension. Ask what these symptoms symbolize and recognize and forgive yourself for your part in creating them. Ask for images to appear of the traumas or negative patterns related to these areas.

4. Do you express both your constrictive and your expansive feelings honestly and appropriately? Practice honest and appropriate ways to express your feeling in a journal, to a friend, or write them out in letters you do not send.

5. When you have an intuitive sense of what the dark shadow of your illness is, then explore what the light, luminous intent of your shadow is by asking yourself these questions: "What does this give me?" "What is even more important than that?" Feel the negativity, without judging it until you arrive at a luminous intent. Under "self-pity," or "control" may be "safety" or "peace." Then ask what does this do to the need to control or self-pity?

Chapter Two

The Body as Soul and Spirit

$\mathcal{T}$he issues the shadow holds for us make us ill, but our encounter and processing of these issues can make us well. Every symptom is an aspect of the shadow that is expressed in our flesh and physical form. Through the symptom we experience what we are refusing to live out on a conscious level. These symptoms force us to live out and embody the very energies and issue we have denied, abandoned and rejected; these symptoms suggest to us what can be recognized, forgiven and changed or accepted and embraced.

Honoring the Body

These shadow symptoms then offer us an opportunity to heal ourselves by mirroring back to us what we need to bring to awareness, process and integrate into our lives. Our dominant culture denies the presence of spirit and soul in our lives. Each of our bodies is physical but also made out of the substance of soul. The body is an expression of our multidimensional existence. It is a mistake to think of our bodies as mere machines that wear out in time. They are not machines, nor are they only physical. No machine can heal itself. No machine can respond to our every emotion, thought or attitude instantaneously as they occur. No machine keeps going when its operator is asleep.

Finally, no machine automatically replaces its own worn out parts. When we live in peaceful ways that supply the physical needs of our bodies, we are naturally healthy. We can trust our bodies to respond to us for they are the creative media of our souls which bring us messages as do our dreams. Illness and suffering are the result of a misdirection of our creative energies and mistaken choices.

The only purpose of suffering and pain is to teach us to make better choices. Suffering is not good for the soul, unless it teaches us to stop suffering. There are better ways to grow and learn than through suffering. We can learn through love, pleasure, safety and wisdom. If we do have the suffering of illness however, we can use it to learn and face the shadow issues it represents.

Awareness of the body is crucial to all forms of genuine spiritual and physical healing, because bringing awareness back to the body anchors the quality of presence. This is true because, while our minds and feelings can wander off, our bodies can only exist in the present moment. This is why spiritual work requires us first to be grounded in our bodies.

It is common for people in modern society to "check out" or "numb out" of an awareness of what is happening to our bodies. To have presence or intensity in the moment involves occupying our bodies in a profound sense of fullness, strength, autonomy and stability. If we have lost this presence, it is replaced by a false sense of persona or personality. Many do not feel parts of their bodies. By developing an awareness of what is occurring within our bodies when a negative ego pattern occurs, we can use these feelings as a signal to relax, breathe deeply and make better choices.

Scientific Proof of the Relationship between Childhood Trauma and Later Illness

Numerous scientific studies have identified emotional patterns that predispose us to illness. One of these is the recent Adverse Childhood Experiences (ACE) Study which is a long term, in depth analysis of more than 17,000 adult San Diego members of Kaiser Permanente, in which researchers matched current health status against 19 categories of adverse childhood experiences a half-century earlier. The study authors found these findings: (1) adverse childhood experiences are common, although they are typically concealed and unrecognized. (2) adverse experience still have a profound effect 50 years later, although now they have evolved from psychosocial experience to organic disease and mental illness (3) Adverse childhood experiences are the main determinant of the United States' health and social well-being.

This study began in 1980 as the result of trying to discover why so many individuals were obese. The medical personnel had not made the association between a history of abuse and obesity until they made detailed interviews with the dropouts of their weight loss programs. For many of these people, obesity was not their deepest problem; obesity was instead their protective solution to problems not before acknowledged. Overweight for both women and men was a way to protect them selves from being vulnerable to social and sexual advances. In the year after one obese woman was raped, she gained over one hundred pounds.

The most important finding from this study are that adverse childhood experiences including physical, emotional and sexual abuse. Dysfunctional families with absent or alcoholic or drug addicted parents were vastly more common than recognized or acknowledged. These adverse childhood experiences were found to have a powerful relation to adult health fifty years later and have a strong correlation to heart disease, diabetes, obesity, alcoholism, and drug abuse. No health professionals in the Kaiser Foundation had previously sought this kind of personal information before, nor even recognized how it was related to subsequent illnesses.

Dr Vincent Felitti who led this study admitted that most physicians would far rather deal with organic disease alone, as it is easier to do so, but that approach also leads to treatment failures and false or inauthentic diagnoses. Dr. Felitti stated that the usual approach to many adult chronic diseases was like the relationship of smoke to fire. For a person unfamiliar with fires, it would be tempting to treat the smoke because that is the most visible aspect of the problems. Fortunately, fire departments have learned long ago to put out fire with water rather than use fans to clear the smoke away. *"What we have learned,"* Dr Felitti concludes, *"in the ACE Study represents the underlying fire in medical practice where we often treat symptoms rather than underlying causes."*

As a result of this study, health professionals in the Kaiser system are now more aware that the primary shadow issues which are the source of illness are well protected by social convention and taboo. Dr. Felitti admits that physicians have limited themselves to a small part of the real origin of physical problems, in part because it is more comfortable to be mere prescribers of medication. In a report of the findings of this study, Dr Felitti asks the question: Who and when should medical professionals treat the deeper issues of adverse childhood experiences that lead to physical illness later in life? This scientific study is important because it reveals the deep issues that lie hidden in the shadow of illness. Health professionals need to be brave and compassionate enough to at last face and heal these issues, because we now know how to approach the fire beneath the smoke of illness.

A Healing Solution for
Asthma given in a Dream

The shadow can give us messages in our dreams to heal ourselves and others. I had the following dream on the night before I was to see John who had heard that I worked with guided imagery and music for healing. I knew little about John before this dream so I was elated to later find that the dream gave me clear indications as to how I was to help him. This was my dream:

I am a worker in a welfare office. There is a family who come in concerning a complaint about the father being treated unjustly. The father is a black man who sits in front of his son who is Hispanic. The son is very upset about the injustice done to his father. On the left is the daughter of the family who rises and begins to act crazily by dumping over waste paper baskets and making a commotion. The thing I do in the dream is to help by giving this daughter a white rob to wear. This seems to help calm the situation. There was a deep feeling of despair in the room before this solution was given.

John was a middle-aged man who suffered from severe bouts of asthma that required frequent hospitalizations and severe sciatic pain in his left hip and leg. He was a poet, yet he said he was unable to visualize. Our work together began by helping John relax and experience and visualize his body. John became aware that nearly half of his body, his left side, felt weak, blank or empty. Through guided imagery and music we were able to identify what pattern of behavior this represented.

John had a conflicted relationship with his father and as a result had denied the side of him that was most alive and vibrant-his creative feminine side and with it his desires to be a writer and poet. John first had to express his great sorrow concerning his relationship with his father. The symptoms of asthma have often been compared to someone who is being smothered or suffocated and so cannot breathe. One of the questions John asked himself was, "What is it that is suffocating or smothered me?" Through the symbolism of his asthma and the sciatic pain, his body presented John with what was in his dark shadow.

John's father was a man who was envious of his brothers who had succeeded in ways he had not been able to achieve. John like his father was driven by envy, shame and rage from feeling weak and less than he wished to be. He believed that there was something fundamentally missing in him that others had that he lacked. This was true as long as he rejected and devalued his own feminine energy by thinking it was dangerous or crazy.

He associated his sciatic pain with a great sadness he felt about his dead father who he thought had "kicked him in the butt" in a metaphorical way by never accepting him. John said his father had experienced many injustices during his life, and had dominated him during his youth. When John was a young man he used street drugs in a dangerous way and his father under the guise of "saving him from drugs" had stepped in and gotten him a job in his own insurance agency. His father had a sad, dejected manner and had died young. Although John no longer used drugs, he felt his spirit had been lost when he had agreed to live the life his father had chosen for him rather than his own.

In the process of his healing, he got in touch with his heart feelings. Through these feelings he reached the strength and fullness of being that comes to us when the false sorrow of our personality agendas is replaced by the genuine desires and feelings of our true selves. It was illuminating how my dream paralleled John's negative ego pattern.

While worked with me, John began to remember and learn from his dreams. His dreams suggested the need to fill in the empty places within himself and to use the tools he had been given. One of the dreams John had during our therapy work was of his father coming to him and showing him a tool shed full of tools and telling him that all of these were his. In the dream,

John refused to accept these tools. He also refused the tools of imagination, desire and intuition, aspects of his anima, essential to his health.

When John took the effort to pay attention to his body, he became aware that not only was there something missing in his body but also a sense of emotional emptiness, sorrow and despair there. The left side of his body, the feminine, imaginative side of himself felt for him empty, weak and in pain. This felt image of his body reflected the fact that his shadow held for him all the imagination, desire and intuition that he had rejected in himself. Gradually John learned to value these feminine tools of creation and discovered his feminine side which opened him to a fuller masculinity and creativity.

THE IMPORTANCE OF BALANCE TO HEALING

When John learned to honor his feminine side more, he was able to feel and resolve the grief and remorse about his lost integrity and creative potential. John had rejected his feminine side to emulate his father. Two years after I counselled him, I contacted him and he reported no more asthma attacks or hospitalizations. When he did have symptoms, they were less severe and he was able to face them and heal quickly. For men, the shadow holds not only all the feminine energy men reject by them, but also their rejected masculine energy. For women, the shadow holds not only all the masculine energy women reject in themselves, but also their rejected feminine energy.

Jung was one of the first psychiatrists to acknowledge that within every man there is an inner woman which he called the Anima and within every woman there is an inner man which he called an Animus. Jung recognized that the Anima of a man also held an inherent element of spirituality because it contained those feminine qualities associated with the source of life-the mother and the Goddess. Modern Jungians have expanded upon Jung's concepts and most agree that men and women each have an inner man and woman. The relationship to our inner woman or man is symbolic of outer relationships with men and women.

If a man fails to accept his feminine energy of desire, imagination and intuition, he in effect emasculates himself because he loses the potential to conceive new ideas and be creative. He is only quite literally half a man; in John's case he would fail to become a successful poet if he refused to accept the feminine side of himself, because the use of imagination is required to become a poet. It was significant that John, who considered himself a poet, was unable to imagine or dream, and this creative blockage was the primary reason he asked me to help him.

The left unhealthy, painful, numb side of his body was symbolized in my dream as the woman who acted crazily by tipping over waste baskets and causing a confusion in my welfare office. I was directed by my dream image to calm her and make her holy by focusing upon what she desired and represented. In the asthmatic symptoms that John experienced, he literally had suffocated his imagination-a vital part of himself that caused him to only be half a man. There are many men and women who deny their feminine energies in our society because imagination, desire and intuition are devalued by our major institutions-our families, religions and educational systems.

Masculine qualities are valued most in our dominant society, and feminine qualities are often demeaned or devalued. With this devaluation also comes an emphasis on competition, comparison and achievement as a means of affirming self esteem through outside validation rather than through the genuine essence of our unique presence or being. Masculine energy is the dynamic energy of action, will and manifestation. Feminine energy is the potential of creativity that uses imagination, desire and intuition.

Each one is crippled without the other. Masculine energy is emasculated without feminine energy. Feminine energy is complementary to masculine energy; each fills up or completes the other. Feminine energy compensates or counterbalances what is missing in masculine energy. Masculine energy acts upon the potential insights that feminine energy possesses. To have a successful creative project, I first become inspired by a meaningful new idea which I then write and give dynamic form upon the page. To be a healthy person, both feminine and masculine energies must function together in a cooperative, creative way to allow an individual to fully express and realize their unique self.

How Illnesses vary with the Personality Changes of Multiples

The adversary of the shadow is the ego personalities and their negative ego agendas. The personality ego denies and rejects the shadow issues, including feminine energy in a man and masculine energy in a woman. John was a man who felt great shame and rage as part of his personality ego. He felt he was only half the man he was meant to be because he had rejected the very thing that could make him whole.

The most dramatic and clear evidence of the relationship between the body and the ego personality is in the lives and health of multiple personalities. Multiple personality disorder is a syndrome in which two or more distinct personalities inhabit a single body. People with this disorder are often not aware that control of their body is being shared by different personalities. Most multiples can have between eight to thirteen personalities. Almost all multiples have a history of severe childhood trauma, often in the form of horrible psychological, physical and sexual abuse.

People who have multiple personalities experience various illnesses with each change of personality. The demonstration of the relationship between personality and the illnesses is instantaneous. As soon as the personality of the individual changes their illnesses also change. What was once in the shadow of the multiple is expressed in one personality but not in another. One personality can be diabetic while another is not. One personality can be allergic to dogs or cats while another is not. One personality can make insulin as it needs it, and in the next moment when the personality changes to another, cannot make insulin. One personality can be allergic to peanuts while another is not.

The disorder of multiples is often related to the shame they experienced as a result of emotional, mental and physical abuse in childhood. To survive such abuse, the abused individual learned to split itself into various personalities in order to dissociate from the experiences that were too painful to otherwise endure. Research upon people with multiple personalities has shown that each personality possesses a different brain-wave pattern. Not only do the brain waves of multiples change, but also their blood flow patterns, muscle tone, heart rate, and posture. In one case all the subpersonalities were allergic to orange juice except one. When that personality took over the body the allergies would instantly start to fade and this man could drink orange juice without symptoms.

Some of the physical symptoms that vary from one personality to the next in multiples include scars, cysts, and left-right handedness. Other physical characteristics that may vary include:

(1) A change in visual acuity which require the multiple to possess several different pairs of glasses
(2) Color blindness
(3) Different voice patterns

(4) One personality can be diabetic while another is not.

(5) Epilepsy can come or go with changes in personality

(6) Each personality of a female multiple can have a different menstrual cycle

(7) When one of the personalities of a multiple is a child, the medications prescribed for adult personalities when taken by this personality is over dosage.

(8) One personality may be allergic to substances in the environment, but when another personality appears this allergic reaction instantly disappears.

Dr. Francine Howland, a Yale psychiatrist told of an amazing incident when a multiple had an allergic reaction to a wasp sting. This multiple showed up for an appointment with his eye completely swollen shut from a wasp sting. When this man changed into another personality that felt no pain, the swelling and pain of the sting immediately disappeared and the eye returned to normal.

The author Michael Talbot observed multiple personalities and concluded what we call "self" forms a hologram self and when a multiple shifts from one personality to a different one this is immediately reflected upon his or her body. The evidence of how the physical symptoms of illness change with the ego personality of multiples is significant to how all people can heal themselves. Not only multiples, but all of us are capable of changing our personalities if we learn to change our core beliefs and their related feelings. Some of our selves can make us ill, some help us heal.

There is considerable evidence, for instance, that a hostile and socially isolated individual is more prone to heart disease. In my own adolescence, during a time when I had much conflict over shyness, I developed one cyst after another upon my neck. Finally I had a cyst removed surgically. I now attribute this condition to my shy personality and inner conflict over wanting to be accepted and at the same time to express my curiosity and intelligence. During the 1950's it was not socially acceptable for a girl to be smart and athletic. As an adolescent, I had a strong urge to be creative and to learn whatever science or literature could teach me about human nature, but suppressed this urge to try to live what was then considered a socially acceptable feminine role.

During our lives we take on many roles with personality changes which affect our bodies. A dramatic example of this was during the time my daughter Leah gave birth to her second child, Aden. Leah and I are close, emotionally and mentally. After this birth, though I was long past my age of menopause, at the age of fifty eight, I began menstruating again. It lasted for two months. I assume that getting swept up emotionally in the role of mother vicariously reactivated the part of me that was a mother. The same phenomena can also be seen when infertile women adopt a child and then miraculously become able to give birth to their own biological children.

Some of the implications of the evidence that comes from multiples of how disease and personality are interrelated are these:

(1) Disease is sourced within the ego personality, specifically its negative ego patterns, not in the physical body alone.

(2) People can heal a disease immediately when a personality change occurs.

(3) We are mistaken to limit our research into the sources or cures of illness to physical matter alone such as genes or chemotherapies.

(4) The sources of disease may very well lie with certain negative ego patterns.

More research needs to be done to identify the relationship between how negative ego emotional-mental patterns such as martyrdom can turn off or on diabetes, and how certain negative ego patterns involving fear of safety and security affect allergies. As a holistic therapist, I have witnessed many healings that came shortly after a patient made dramatic changes in his or her emotional-mental patterns. One dramatic example is changing a worrying, controlling attitude to a more accepting, less controlling one. I once counselled a woman named Patty who had suffered from I.B.S. (irritable bowel syndrome) for years.

Patty had been treated both by traditional and naturopathic means with little relief. What concerned Patty the most in her life was worry over a son Bruce who was a young adult. She tried to control him in various ways because she felt he was making unwise choices and living a life-style she considered unproductive. I asked her to consider whether her control and worry had benefitted either her or Bruce. Patty came to see how her habit of control and worry contributed to her irritable bowel syndrome. Three weeks later Patty had none of her irritable bowel symptoms. She had let go of the personality of the worrier and controller and with it her irritable bowel syndrome.

In the shadow of people with multiple personalities is their shame that can manifest itself in disease in various forms. I once counselled a woman who with the help of another counselor had been able to integrate her various personalities, yet she had problems with her sexuality and a lingering sense of guilt and shame. I was able to help her deal with her shame through helping her write and destroy her shame contracts with those who had abused her. Through the use of imagery, we were able to collect the shame from her sexual body to return it in the form of a slimy bag of shame to the person who had given it to her. Her guilt was processed through expressing the anger beneath it in anger letters that were later destroyed. As a result of this work her sexual relationship with her husband improved and she was able to let go of some of her feelings of envy and jealousy to allow herself to receive things she had before felt she did not deserve. The enneagram is a tool that we can use to help us recognize our dark shadow issues and the light shadows beneath them.

THE SACRED PSYCHOLOGY OF THE ENNEAGRAM AND THE SHADOW

The enneagram is a geometric figure that maps out the nine fundamental personality types of human nature and their complex interrelationships. The word enneagram comes from the Greek for nine-"ennea." The enneagram is a nine pointed figure within the diagram of a circle that indicates the directions of our integration or disintegration of our personality drives. The enneagram is a valuable tool to help us bridge the gap between psychology and the metaphysics of spirituality and religion. The enneagram is part of an ancient tradition sourced in the spiritual wisdom of ancient Christianity, and the religious traditions of the East (especially the Sufis) which has been clarified by modern thinkers.

Riso and Russell have contributed to the tradition of the enneagram by defining the healthy, average, and unhealthy levels of each enneagram personality type. These men realized the without spirituality, psychology cannot free us and lead us to our true selves. Yet, without psychology, spirituality can lead us into delusion, escapism and grandiosity. Each personality type becomes unhealthy in certain predictable ways. Peacemakers for instance disintegrate by abandoning themselves and only wanting "peace" without acknowledging the need to confront conflict with courage and to stand up for their own interests and rights.

We all have these nine main drives that could motivate us, but one of these is our primary drive, the one we would choose first if we were backed into a corner and told we could choose only one. We also have another secondary drive upon which we often depend or lean. My main drive is that of a peacemaker, but I also lean upon the reformer. When we understand our personality negative ego drives and the predictable way these drives get out of balance, we can help ourselves and others know what attitudes and errors cause us to be unhealthy. Psychological integration and spiritual realization are not separate processes. We disintegrate and integrate in certain specific healthy and unhealthy ways, depending upon our primary and secondary drives.

At the core of the study of the enneagram is the truth that our basic personality drive reveals the psychological negative ego agendas or strategies by which we forget our true nature-our true Self and Divine Essence. Our personalities or personas with their negative ego patterns then shield and defend us in order to survive our childhoods. These personality drives become automatic ways of thinking, feeling and behaving that make up the core of our personalities and prevent us from having a direct experience of our true selves or Essence.

The loss of contact with our Unique Selves causes deep anxiety and what the enneagram calls the nine passions or sins. These basically are the negative ego agendas or strategies our personality ego selves used to survive our wounds, and the less than ideal conditions of our childhoods. By bringing our attention to the present moment, we begin to be filled with a new sense of unique self, separate from our negative ego personality self.

This self or presence knows and can reveal to us what is preventing us from being more present. The more we become present in our true Self, the more we become aware of the parts of us that are tense, defensive and negative. By becoming aware of the false strategies, passions and mistaken agendas of our personality egos that cause us to disintegrate and thus be unhealthy, we can reject and refuse to act upon them.

The negative ego strategy of my personality drive as a peacemaker is one that tells me, "You don't matter. You have no voice in this matter." The negative ego strategy of my lean the reformer #1 tells me, "Don't act because you may make a mistake." Once I identified the underlying lie of these negative ego strategies, I can reject them. I integrate when I move toward achievement, and disintegrate when I seek only safety and refuse to take risks and be courageous. My true self is deeply caring and concerned with what truly matters to me, my clients and the people around me who I love. I can listen to negative ego agendas that my dark shadow holds, but in my awareness of their darkness, I do not act on them.

THE ENNEAGRAM

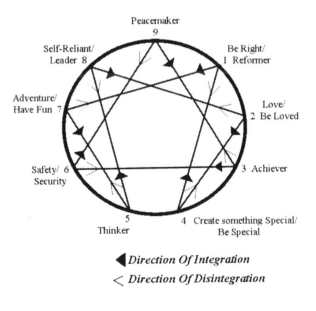

◄ *Direction Of Integration*

< *Direction Of Disintegration*

Figure 2

NEGATIVE EGO PERSONALITY DRIVE
ERRORS HELD IN THE SHADOW

Our shadows hold for us the passions, sins or mistakes of our negative egos agendas until we are ready to heal them. The passions or sins of the enneagram are the main ways we lose our balance and are distorted in our thinking, feeling and doing. If we know these negative ego mistakes, we can listen and reject them as the unsuccessful ways we survived childhood, but as temptations we are smarter and stronger now to resist:

(1) The passion of the **reformer** is **anger or resentment**. Reformers tend to deny their rage, anger and resentment.

(2) The passion of the **lover** is **pride or vain glory** in one's virtue or a refusal to accept that their behavior is less than loving.

(3) The passion of the **achiever** is **deceit or vanity** in its attempt to replace genuine spirituality with some other worldly achievement.

(4) The passion of the **creative of the special** person is **envy** based on the feeling that something fundamental is missing or flawed in them that others have that they are lacking.

(5) The passion of the **thinker** is **avarice** or the feeling that they lack the inner resources to cope in the world and to interact with others because of their own limited resources, so must minimize their needs and relationships.

(6) The passion of the **safety-security** person is **anxiety,** the constant apprehension or worry about possible threats that can occur in the future.

(7) The passion of the **adventurer** is gluttony or the insatiable desire to be filled with new adventures or experiences that are never enough.

(8) The passion of the **leader** is a constant need for **intensity, control and self extension** over others or their environment.

(9) The passion of **peacemakers** is that of **sloth** in their unwillingness to rise up or engage fully and vitally with life.

We need our personality egos to give us information of what is happening in our immediate environment. With an awareness of the repetitive messages of our negative ego, we can choose not to identify with these lesser aspects of ourselves. We can become more aware of the positive side of our drives and let go of the automatic self defeating agendas that our drives suggest to us. The small agendas of our personality drives can be compared to the owner of a beautiful mansion choosing to live in one of its dark closets when he could choose to enjoy the beauty and pleasure of the entire mansion.

Spiritual Pain in Relationship to Illness

Our dominant culture and medical tradition denies the presence of spirit and soul within our bodies. Just as the Divine conscious is in our minds it is also within our bodies and repairs the body continuously. Disease can occur when there is interference or blockage of information from our energetic to our cellular levels. Soul and spirit are both inside and outside of the body. We can directly encounter our shadow-souls in meditation successfully when we take some important precautions.

Since our souls are more concerned with our mental, emotional and spiritual growth than they are with our physical bodies, this does not mean our shadows are evil or negative. Our shadows value our lasting spiritual and emotional growth more than the temporary well being of our physical bodies. For this reason it is always important when we are doing work with our shadows *to ask our higher selves* or inner guides to interpret their messages to us.

The shadow is a face of our souls, so despite its ominous appearance it loves us as our soul does, but wishes us to grow and heal in all ways. If in meditation, we ask our shadow what it needs to make peace and are told, "Your heart," then we need to ask our higher selves to tell us what this means. If our higher self says, "No, don't give that," we need to listen, because our shadow may be literally meaning that by having a heart attack, we would be at peace. We then can reply, "No, what else do you need from me to make peace with you."

"What do I need to let go or do to heal ----?" and

"What do you hold of mine that I need to heal----?"

Our higher self or inner counselors know better than we how to interpret the symbolic language of our shadows. Since the shadow is part of our souls, it speaks a metaphoric language which sees our body and its parts in symbolic ways. The left side of the body, for instance, often represents the feminine or receptive side that needs to awaken to a new level of strength for us to become whole and to reach the level of spiritual growth and life purposes we wish to achieve.

Our Souls are infinite but also temporarily physical. They do not need the physical to exist. We do not have to be conscious to breathe, or to digest food, or to regeneration a stomach or liver. The unconscious mind, the most conscious part of us, is closest to our souls and the functioning of our bodies. This soul energy continuously controls our autonomic bodily functions such as breathing, circulating blood, and digesting food. These are all spontaneous processes that if we are healthy need no conscious control. Soul is a feminine energy that is the substance of our life.

This substance of soul communicates with our autonomic nervous system in response to the energy and breath of spirit.

Spirit is a masculine energy that gives us inspiration and dynamic energy to achieve. Spirit stirs soul to heal through conscious intention that leads to unconscious creation. Our spirits can be diminished and nearly killed, but our souls are always with us. Nothing can measure soul and spirit, but we can experience both in our bodies and minds.

Certain feelings and perspectives attract more of soul and spirit to us. More of our soul is attracted to us whenever we are feeling a **beautiful sadness** such as when saying goodbye to a loved one, or when we feel **tender, gentle, passionate, courageous, confident and joyous**. More of our spirit is attracted to us when we feel **powerful, free, loving, valued, aligned and know we are good enough.**

More specifically spiritual pain is related to seventh chakra issues particular located at the crown of the head which affects the nervous system, muscles, skin and skeletal structure. Some of the negative emotional patterns that interfere with the health of the seventh chakra are living a meaningless life, an absence of faith, feeling unsupported, an absence of courage or faith in oneself, a fear of self-development, a lack of wisdom to see the pattern of your life, or a lack of vision beyond your personal needs. Some of the diseases that result from these kinds of issues are nervous system issues such as multiple sclerosis, paralysis, bone cancer and amyotrophic lateral sclerosis or (ALS)

RESPONSIBILITY AND HEALING
SHADOW ISSUES

Our roles in creating and healing an illness lead to the questions of responsibility. None of us directly or deliberately cause an illness but we do create the emotional, mental environments in which illnesses occur. Without owning our part in developing an illness we are powerless against it. Responsibility is essential to power and to the freedom from illness. In our culture we have focused only on the negative side of responsibility for illness without seeing the positive side which is better health. If there is a run down house, you cannot fix or change it unless you own it. Without owning it, you have no responsibility to change it. The power to heal ourselves lies in owning an illness as ultimately our responsibility, and thus taking back the power to heal it.

The common idea that some illnesses are psychosomatic and others are not has been challenged by the holistic health movement that assumes that body and mind are always interconnected, either in good health or illness. The popular idea that the center of healing is the physician is one that needs to be resisted. Some physicians are trustworthy and some are not. Before beginning a treatment that may be harmful to us, it is important to do research about this treatment or find someone who can do the research for us.

One of the most blatant examples of the misuse of the authority of physicians was their advocacy of hormone replacement therapy to a whole generation of women. A large number of women of my generation might not have experienced breast cancer, if there had not been an aggressive campaign by drug companies and doctors to advocate the use of hormone replacement. Responsibility for our health means we accept whatever helpful treatment methods both traditional and alternative are available to us, and avoid known cacogenics, drugs or alcohol that would harm us.

Spiritual healing is freedom from the tyranny of suffering. We know we have reached this kind of freedom when we come to a peaceful place within that does not depend upon something outside ourselves. To find this peace and healing requires us to honestly feel the sorrow, grief, or pain involved in our suffering. Then we need to forgive ourselves and the others involved to transmute our pain. We can then release the hidden agendas and negative ego beliefs and feelings that keep us stuck in our suffering, particularly those of blame, guilt or self punishment. This suffering can then be replaced by a more open, receptive, accepting and nonviolent attitude.

One of the reasons people do not wish to take responsibility for the creation of an illness is they assume they will have to blame themselves and then suffer more from this blame. Blame is placing a negative judgment against the self or others. Taking responsibility does not need to make such a judgment; taking responsibility begins when you recognize whatever negative ego personality patterns contributed to its creation.

Ellen suffered from hyperthyroidism and refused to accept the traditional treatment of this illness which she found extreme- the radiation of her thyroid gland which would kill it. She realized that much of the environment which created this disease was the result of her assuming the entire emotional weight of her family while her husband was being unfaithful and neglectful to her and her family. When she divorced him, she began to consider her own needs for growth and happiness, and her thyroid returned to a normal level.

SHADOW WORK EXERCISES-CHAPTER TWO

(1) List the physical symptoms of your illness or illnesses. Then reflect upon your negative ego personality patterns when you experienced these symptoms. What negative belief do you have related to this illness?

(2) What were your main feelings and thoughts during these illnesses?

(3) What was out of balance in the thoughts and feelings related to these personalities? What lies did your negative ego tell you?

(4) What enneagram passion is related to this negative ego personality pattern? Was it sloth, deceit, pride, lust, anger, envy, fear or gluttony or avarice?

(5) Where in childhood were you traumatized or abused sexually, mentally or emotionally?

(6) To survive this trauma, what strategy did you use? How do you soothe yourself? What do you do now to soothe yourself or to feel safe?

(7) In meditation, visit these experiences from a higher perspective to talk to your inner child, or adolescent to touch them with love and explain why these strategies don't work and how they can be replaced by healthier ones.

(8) Remember moments of spiritual awakening when you felt safe and loved. Touch the traumatized parts of your self with this love.

Chapter Three

Our Bodies as Reflections
of Our Pain

J believe that emotional memories of painful childhood experiences are stored in the body and get passed on to other cells over time until they are recognized, felt, forgiven and resolved. As a holistic healer with years of experience working with people who have painful memories hidden under their illnesses, I know that it is essential not just to cure the physical symptoms, but to discover what it is this illness is trying to convey. The first step of healing painful memories is in a relaxed state to focus upon their bodily symptoms and to inquire what emotional memories and patterns they represent.

HEALING OF TERMINAL CANCER

Years ago, I was asked to work with a woman named Joyce, I used imagery and music to help her heal and forgive the anger that had manifested in cancer throughout her body. Joyce had received counselling from others, but she had not been able to release and forgive the righteous blame and anger beneath her cancer. Joyce blamed her cancer upon her ex-husband and family. Joyce however was willing to look at where on her body she carried this anger; she recognized this anger was related to the cancer in her body. With the help of imagery and music, Joyce identified numerous places on her body this anger was held and she described their color and shape. I asked her if she was willing to release these angers by reaching into her body and placing them in a transforming cauldron in the middle of a forest. Joyce with great feeling released all of these angers to the cauldron except one. This anger was at her throat and represented unspoken anger. We asked for a wise mentor; Joyce chose Jesus and with his help she was later able to say what she needed to say to resolve her anger. I later learned that Joyce's cancer had gone into "remission" shortly after I worked with her.

WE NEED TO FEEL TO HEAL

Our emotions are the doorway to the light and joy of healing that lies under the darkness of illness. It is essential in healing that the ill individuals **feel** the suppressed painful emotions such as anger, shame, hurt, apathy, fear, loneliness, lethargy, disappointment or despair that are there. This does not mean they have to wallow in the feeling, but that they need to spend the time it takes to feel these emotions with intensity. These feelings are often repressed or suppressed because they are painful and are not accepted by our parents or others. We are often taught to deny, distract, or reject these feelings as unimportant or unacceptable to ourselves. Our rational egos often deny the importance of emotional reactions because these feelings are neither comfortable nor familiar. These shadow feelings also give us an excuse and permission not to do more, to hide, or to deny that healing is possible, so they go into our shadow, body and subconscious.

CHRONIC STRESS AS A REFLECTION OF PAIN

Many people assume that to be responsible, they need to accept being stressed. Too many of us believe if we are to succeed we have to live in a hectic, struggling and competitive way with little space or time for contemplation, spirit or cooperation. This imbalance fosters an unhealthy, chronic stressfulness with too much yang or negative masculine energy which fosters a devaluation of more nurturing, feminine (not female) ways of living. This driven, "nose to the grindstone" life-style affects both women and men in unhealthy ways, such as one that considers struggle, competition and perfectionism as at least a necessity, and at best a noble life style.

The price paid for a chronically stressed life-style is often illness. Chronic stress leads to immune suppression and immune dysfunctional illness. Some of the long term unhealthy consequences of chronic stress are cardiomyopathy, digestive disorders, immune suppression, impaired insulin regulation and damage to the hippocampus which controls our cognitive/ emotional life. We do not yet know the cause of cancer, but we do know that the immune systems of people who get cancer have probably been compromised in some significant way.

Imagined and real fear manifests the same reaction in our physical bodies. Most of the sources of our stress come from inner threats rather than outer dangers in our environment. The fear of loss of power, loss of our basic needs, loss of intimacy, or the loss of our real self can have the same bodily reactions as if we really were meeting a tiger in the jungle. When we are in the stress reaction of "flight or fight" our immune and reproductive systems become less active. All of the energy goes to muscles and organs that will help us escape. It helps to diffuse some of the threat of that source by understanding what it is that is threatened.

Consider the consequences of not dealing with the fear that lies beneath chronic stress such as going into the shadow of denial, distraction or discounting your fear. What illness threatens? Once you have determined this, commit yourself to learn what the pattern is behind your fear. Are you afraid of the future, dependent on others for safety, or afraid of being uncomfortable or confused? Write a fear letter to yourself, being specific about all the things you fear, state where this fear began, and why you have decided to hang on to it.

Underneath depression and despair are many small angers that you think will get you in trouble if they are expressed. Under despair may be guilt that is anger you think you have no right to. If you are depressed or guilty, admit it. Then express this anger and/or guilt honestly and appropriately. Chronic depression is not only unpleasant, it is dangerous. It weakens the immune system and destroys its power to protect our bodies against malignant growths and disease.

TRAUMA AND STRESS AS A SOURCE OF ILLNESS

Traumatic events or experiences are always stressful, but stressful events can be traumatic only if we perceive them to be. Traumatic events are those that people suffer from when they perceive these experiences as life threatening or overwhelming. The word "traumatic" is sometimes used as a synonym for stressful as when someone says, "My day was traumatic" to describe the ordinary stresses of their life. All stressful events are not traumatic. The events that are traumatic however are those that give us clues or information concerning our dark shadows and the negative ego issues they hold for us.

The traumatic events of our lives are those which we most often ignore, deny, misunderstand and eventually become sources of illness. No two people are alike in what to them is traumatic. There are many factors involved in how someone may respond to a threatening event. The response of an individual to a potential threat can depend upon their previous history of trauma, genetic makeup, or family dynamics. It is essential to respect these differences in ourselves and others so we can approach what we each perceive as traumatic in a compassionate, hopeful way.

A traumatic experience differs from a stressful one because at the center of every traumatic experience is the pain of losing our connection to our bodies, to ourselves, to our families, and to the world around us. A trauma can impact us in ways that do not show up until years later. A loss of connection can occur slowly and gradually so it is often difficult to recognize that it is happening.

With the loss of connection comes a gradual constriction of our freedom and natural well being. Children and adolescences are particularly vulnerable to traumatic experiences, because they are more easily overwhelmed when they do not understand what is happening around them. A series of threatening experiences can be just as overwhelming to a child or adolescent as one catastrophic event.

Traumatic events disconnect people from their bodies as if their feet and legs were pulled out from under them. There is a loss of a feeling of safety and security (first chakra issues) that can lead to physical symptoms or illness. Healing requires a process of reconnecting with our inner and outer sources of support to regain a sense of well being again. Triggering events that can be traumatic are car accidents, medical procedures, the loss of a loved one, a natural disaster, or a forced move.

Hardiness as a Way of Coping with Stress and Avoiding Illness

What is considered traumatic and thus stressful to one individual may be for others considered just stressful, or merely a challenge which can be an adventure. In the early 1980's a researcher named Kobasa and her associates did a series of research studies to determine the relationship of stress to illness. The population she studied was a group of highly stressed executives. Her prediction that the executives who had the most illnesses would be those who had the least ability to cope with stress proved to be true.

She identified three qualities: commitment, challenge, and control over a situation that she determined differentiated those who were "hardy" or resilient in the face of stress from those who were not. These hardy or resilient executives also were the ones who had less illness. Kobasa successfully predicted which executives would become ill later in their careers as a result of their low coping abilities in the face of stress.

Two examples of this are George and Mitchell, both executive, who were caught up in their companies' decision that they each needed to relocate. George, who was committed to the life he had chosen within the company, maintained a positive attitude. He chose to see the changes required of him as part of his life purpose. As a result of his hardy resilience, George benefitted from the change and remained healthy.

Arthur, another executive saw the changes as a loss of his power and felt victimized by them. He did not like the climate where he was asked to move and due to this attitude did not befriend his co-workers. He had his first heart attack during an argument with one of the other executives in his new office.

Kobasa defined "control" as power in rather than power over. When we have control in a situation we accept change as a challenge but do not allow that change to destroy the integrity of the unique individual we are. A hardy executive believed he could create his own situation during the transfer. The less hardy executive felt overwhelmed or controlled by the changes required. The most important finding of Kobasa's research team was their conclusion that it was the perception of the change that determined whether or not the stress was overwhelming (or traumatic) and thus a source of illness.

HEALING NEGATIVE EGO ISSUES
RELATED TO ILLNESS

There are two ways to heal chronic stress. The first of these is to change the source of our stress and the second is to change our response to it. Both means of healing begin by listening and becoming aware of what is happening to our bodies. Another consequence of chronic stress is muscular contraction in which our muscles become armored in reaction to a perceived threat. This muscular tension can lead to pain and fatigue. The core of every illness or physical symptom is a real pain that has been pushed down into the body by our subconscious and unconscious minds. In searching for the patterns and experiences that cause illness, it is important to address the part of us that is our negative ego. It is often angry, hidden, manipulative, immature and ugly. The goal is to honestly listen to its destructive agenda for your life, and then to let it know you will no longer allow its negativity to control and ruin your life. This negative ego is the enemy that can kill, cripple or allow you to be ill.

Brenda, a young woman, who was a talented writer, I once counselled, was recovering from a life threatening addiction to drugs. Ugly cysts began appearing on her face during her teenage years. These cysts began at a time she learned she could manipulate her wealthy parents to get the money to purchase and use drugs. Brenda was aware these cysts symbolized her inability to face her manipulative, hurtful drug habits.

For ten years, Brenda had one ugly, pussy cyst after another upon her forehead, jaw, neck and face. Each of these cysts had to be removed surgically. Brenda was an attractive young woman and these cysts made her self-conscious and prevented her from getting the admiration she desired. Under her drug addiction, was a negative ego pattern of lying and manipulating her parents and others to get money, adventure and pleasure. It was not until she had a psychotic break during a withdrawal from drugs that she woke up to the destructive impact her drug addiction had caused.

This awakening was helped by the presence of a Haitian practical nurse, who happened to be cleaning her hospital room. She told Brenda about the struggle she had to come to America and make a living for her family. This nurse bluntly accused Brenda of squandering her privileged life as a wealthy, American who had been given every advantage. This confrontation had an impact and as a result Brenda began to face her negative ego. She imagined it as a bratty little girl who got whatever she wanted by making a fuss or lying.

When Brenda learned to say "No" to the demands of her negative ego, and began using her power as a leader in positive ways, her facial cysts disappeared. She began to face her shadow agenda of manipulating others and became more honest and less hurtful to others. She realized she had been getting a high from controlling others through manipulation, as well as from drugs.

THE WOUNDING OF OUR SOULS

When Brenda explored how she was wounded as a teenage, she remembered an incident in which she had taken her report card from her expensive private school out of the mail box, so her parents could not see how she was failing. She believed that her mother was so involved in an unhappy marriage she did not have the energy, love or courage to confront her with her self-destructive, drug abuse. Her wounding was the belief that her parents were so involved in their own unhappy relationship that they did not notice or love her enough to deal with her manipulative behavior. Brenda learned how to manipulate by watching the interaction between her parents. Her mother used guilt to get what she wanted from her father.

To heal her pain, Brenda first wrote out her painful story. Then I asked her to begin where she had the awakening to how she was wasting her precious life when she nearly died of a drug overdose. I asked her to imagine how she could create a life for herself in which she found and used her talents as a writer and leader. In this story, she was to imagine using her power in honest, direct ways to heal and give her life story a happy ending.

Another healing exercise, I suggested she could do was to dialogue, both in meditation and in her journal, with her negative ego by giving it a platform to tell her what its destructive agenda was for her life. Then she was to thank it for helping her survive her childhood and adolescence, but then to tell this bratty girl, negative ego why this no longer worked for her and what was the more positive plans she had for her life.

Brenda then was to stand where her negative ego-the bratty kid had stood and to take back all the energy, imagination and goodness this negative ego had stolen from her. She imagined this kid being transformed into a more mature, cooperative ego. This transformed ego would no longer be focused upon getting her way and getting "high" through manipulating others or through using drugs.

TYPES OF PAIN

Pain is a current of energy, the sensation produced when there is both a yearning for, and a separation from the human needs of security, survival, belonging, esteem and creativity-productivity that happens at the same moment. Real pain is not only physical but emotional, mental, and spiritual.

- Physical pain responses to issues of survival, security and belonging. It often occurs when we are separated and longing for control and a way to feel alive.
- Mental pain occurs when we long to have it all make sense. This pain responds to the need to know, grow, have beauty, and to do things differently.
- Emotional pain responds to a need to work, belong, create and be productive. It responds to the separation and longing to belong. This pain comes when we are separate from but want to feel our existence matters and that we belong to something.
- Spiritual pain is a feeling of emptiness and hollowness when there is a longing for and a separation from a relationship with the Divine. This pain responds to the esoteric need for beauty, balance, and a relationship with the Divine.

Pain is an ally because it alerts us to where we need to grow and change. Pain does not go away by only venting or releasing emotions, because it is a current of energy that needs to be resolved through awareness and change. There is a process of healing pain which begins with consciously choosing to heal the source of our real pain. To heal our pain, it is necessary to start with the present to find the current or flow of energy and determine what its common denominator is. To trace where this current began, we need to explore the lesser selves such as our child, adolescent, or negative ego.

HEALING THE NEGATIVE EGO
PATTERNS OF MULTIPLE SCLEROSIS

Ginny was a forty-four year old married, elementary school teacher who I began working with in the summer of 1994. She had been diagnosed as having Multiple Sclerosis three years earlier. She believed she was in a temporary "grace period" as the doctors expected she would get worse and would eventually become an invalid. Her symptoms were tiredness, a drooping, numb right cheek, numbness on her right side at intervals, and slurred speech. We worked together intensively for six months processing her illness to discover and heal the messages it gave her. Part of the work we did was to create a healing tape Ginny later used on a regular basis to engage her subconscious in a holistic way to heal the issues we discovered together. This tape gave her permission to express all her feelings, including her anger and fear; it encouraged her to pursue her goals with passion and integrity.

Six years later, I contacted Ginny and she told me she had no symptoms of M.S. She attributed her healing to the intensive work we did together in 1994. She had taken none of the new medications that were reported to be helpful for M.S., because her symptoms had disappeared. During our work together, we discovered the image she held of her illness was of "a tight rubber band." From this image, we both concluded that the origin of her illness was her controlling or dominating negative ego, a third chakra power-control issue. We also discovered that Ginny's greatest fear was she would be selfish. As a result of this fear, her focus of attention was upon pleasing others, especially her husband, Dan. Closely related to this attitude was the fear that she would be unloved.

Ginny's greatest personality drive, according to the enneagram system, was that of the lover with a lean upon the achiever. Ginny was driven to control herself in an attempt to gain love. Her greatest fear was of being unworthy of love. Her basic desire to be loved had deteriorated into the need to be needed. Although her principal drive was that of a lover, Ginny got approval by being an achiever.

To be needed, Ginny abandoned and martyred herself for the interests of others, especially to those of her narcissistic husband. She "got on her own nerves" literally. This pattern had been learned from a stoical mother who deferred and protected her father. After her father had a nervous breakdown, her mother protected him from emotional involvement with his children. His needs were considered more important than his children's.

The negative ego patterns of Ginny's multiple sclerosis focused on Ginny accepting a devalued, position based upon placing her own interests secondary to those of her husband's. This chauvinistic life-style caused her rage and resentment. Instead of living her own life spontaneously, just as her mother had done with her father, Ginny stoically deferred to Dan's desires.

In assessing how she was imbalanced, Ginny believed that in focusing upon the needs of others, she had set up an inner environment of resentment and rage in herself. She felt she had too much negative masculine energy. The impossible promise of this position was, "If you are sweet and nice, and get peoples' approval, you will be loved and happy." The antidote to this would be to bring in more of the feminine energy of intuition and love to balance her self-neglect.

Obviously, her agenda of pleasing others had not worked. If she focused only on others, they were blamed and resented when she was sick or unhappy. Her healing fulcrum issue was to focus upon self-love and love of others to balance her misdirected focus upon getting approval. Instead of knowing and acting upon her own goals and interests, she had become a pawn to the interests of her husband. Since he had suffered a heart attack several years before, Ginny felt he was entitled to special care, as her father had. Ginny's belief system was affected by her earlier Mormon religious beliefs. These had encouraged her to see self-love as selfishness and the interests of men as above those of women. Ginny was able to resolve this chauvinistic belief system in her mind, by realizing an important truth: We cannot love others purely and cleanly, without resentment or anger, if we do not first love ourselves. The old quote, "Do onto others, as you would do onto yourself," has as its fulcrum word "as." If we are unwilling to love ourselves, we will be unable to love others because of feelings of resentment and anger.

MY WOUNDING

My pain has been a creative blockage that stops me from fully manifesting, completing and being as creative and productive as I wished to be. At the base of this pain is the delusion that "I do not matter, so neither do my creations." This delusion originated from the wound of my thirteen year old adolescent self who nearly bled to death when I first started menstruating. This was a soul wounding that took some of my passion for life. The message I got as a thirteen year old was, "I really did not matter as a young woman, if my mother, in her shame and powerlessness would allow me to bleed to death." What accompanied this belief and shame was the powerlessness of rage.

The wound each of us experiences in our adolescence is a soul wound that separates us from our spirituality and cultural programs so we can give birth to our individual selves. Through this wound, we experience a mental rebirth that separates us from our parents. After this wounding, we enter our shadow years in which we have thirty or more years to find the individual selves we need to become to give birth to ourselves. I needed to separate from my parent's pattern of fear, shame and a religiosity that denied my basic sexual-creative potential.

Healing my soul wound was done by forgiving my mother for why she had failed to be there to help me understand what was happening to me as I began menstruating and to help me recognize when my body was not functioning well in the process. This was not possible for my mother because of her own inhibitions concerning sexuality. My mother came from a large, religious family in which she also was not taught to understand her own sexuality and to honor it as a natural, positive process.

There are many ways to handle pain, by denying, distracting, discounting or mobilizing it. We can make light of our pain, distance ourselves from it, or become obsessive-compulsive, extremely angry, have addictions, be fearful about many things, become hypercritical, numb ourselves, or hurt others. I dealt with my pain by numbing myself and by mobilizing my attempts to prove I did matter through struggle. To heal myself, I had to recognize my real pain, own it-by assuming responsibility for it, and forgive myself and my mother. To forgive my mother, I recognized my mother was raised in a large, religious family of ten children where she was taught sexuality was shameful and she was powerless to deal with her sexual self.

An important step in my healing was making what was in my subconscious and unconscious, conscious so I could understand it and heal myself. As a teenager this pain manifested as a large cyst on the right side of my neck which was frequently drained of fluids and finally removed surgically. This pain later manifested itself as hypothyroidism during my mid-life crises when I worked to heal a goiter in my neck by empowering myself to express myself more and working directly with my subconscious mind. I recognized that the subconscious wanted to expel and be rid of my pain by shoving it down into various parts of my body. The mind moves pain down and in, and the subconscious tries to expel it by moving it up and out, and shoving it down into the unconscious and body where it can cause illness.

Hypothyroidism involves an autoimmune disease in which the thyroid is being attacked and there is too little thyroid hormone being produced. As a result of this deficiency, the body is tired and lacks energy. As with any autoimmune disease, it is important to look at how defensive or defenseless the woman feels about expressing herself. Healing of this rage occurs when a woman begins identifying her anger and allowing herself to express it. Rage is a form of powerlessness, so expressing the anger can begin to show her how this expression is powerful. There is always a fear involved when there is a feeling of powerlessness, but this fear can gradually be overcome when a woman begins to experience her own ability to impact those around her in a positive way.

Merely treating the symptoms of low thyroid does not heal the thyroid itself; it can even lead to a greater deficiency in its functioning when it fools the body into thinking it is producing enough thyroid. What heals the thyroid, rather than merely cures its symptoms, is for a woman to empower herself to speak, write and express all of her feelings. If she waits for her partner to give her this permission, she may wait forever. The spiritual forces of the universe have already given her permission to express herself honestly and appropriately.

To heal herself, a woman has to give herself this permission for no one else can give it to her. When there is some form of mental, emotion or sexual abuse involved, a woman may need to realize she is punishing herself when she continues to be in an abusive relationship. To heal my pain, I went into the subconscious to meet a personification of my subconscious to dialogue and change its rules. The subconscious is subjective and can be seen as a labyrinth, an underground cave, a library, a high-tech laboratory. My subconscious is a library and the head librarian was only too willing to help me. I thanked her for her past help in dealing with my pain, but told her I was changing my rules. I told her I wanted her to take the energy of my pain and find a new, positive formation for it. I also found new trust in life I needed to be healthy and creative.

TRANSFORMING OUR PAINFUL STORIES

Some of the warnings or clues that you may be in pain are when you are drawn to violence and sorrow. Another clue is when you are self-punishing and judgmental of yourself and others. If you are numbing your feelings, are exhausted, and have insomnia, or isolate yourself from others, these are warning signs that you may be in pain. Pain often wears the masks of depression, anxiety, loneliness, obsessions, false pride, and having many physical injuries.

To begin to heal your pain, set aside a period of time, two or three hours, in which you either write out or tell a friend or counselor what your pain is. Prepare ahead of time to treat yourself in some way through food, music or entertainment after you have done this. Be as honest as possible by giving them the facts as to what your pain is and how you do it. In writing or telling your story, identify its themes or core beliefs, patterns of behavior and the emotions that inevitably flow from these.

Then ask yourself: What is the cost of this story? What did I lose of my health, talent, creativity, imagination, success, happiness, love or energy by living this story? Forgive yourself for the reason you lived this story, by recognizing that when you choose to live it, it gave you freedom and a way to cope with and survive the circumstances of your childhood or young adulthood. Then rewrite this story giving it a happy ending in which you are both happy and more healthy.

In this story act upon those aspects of yourself that you had previously lost while you were living your old, unhealthy story. If your old story was that of the person who now has cancer and you realize that you were a perfectionist who lived in constant anxiety least you be less than perfect, allow yourself to be more accepting. Also allow yourself to focus upon nurturing yourself, having more fun, and being more spontaneous and creative. When you have done this, make it into a myth, beginning with "Once upon a time, there was a beautiful child." As part of this myth, tell what happened to you, what your pain was, and how you healed it. Always give your myth a happy ending, how you healed this pain and lived happily ever after. Then reward yourself by playing your music, eating your special food, and experiencing your entertaining activity.

Another way to heal pain is in meditation to go back to the time your pain began and become the person you were then who experienced it. Then let your spiritual counselors or higher self reach into your body and take it from you. You can also place your pain in a candle and burn it away, or dream it away by wrapping it around a stone which you touch your chakras and say, "Tonight I dream away my pain."

HEALING THE PAIN OF CARPAL TUNNEL TENDONITIS

When I began helping Lisa who had tendonitis pain in her forearms, she felt it as a throbbing, big, round pain that filled and enveloped her right arm. When Lisa relaxed and breathed into this pain, she observed it, and she noticed the quality of her pain changed to a more aching feeling. Pains have a quality to them such as burning, aching, shooting, pressure, throbbing or itching. They also have a volume or shape that can be observed and can change. Lisa's pain became smaller as she observed, relaxed and breathed into it.

The directions for doing a body scan are as follows: Close your eyes. Let your body relax. Make yourself comfortable. Pick an area of discomfort and focus upon it. Notice its size, volume and the quality of the pain there. Get a clear sense of the size, shape and feeling of this pain. Lisa felt her pain as red hot and throbbing. Her pain was more intense near her elbow and her thumb and less intense in the middle of her arm.

As she breathed and relaxed she focused upon cooling this intense, hot throbbing pain by bringing a cool, blue energy to it as she breathed out and relaxed. She breathed out the hot inflamed energy and breathed in cooling blue energy. Lisa noticed that her pain had sharp edges and that it was also present along her lower back and abdomen where she had a skiing accident. When our therapy session ended, Lisa's pain was diminished.

Carpal tunnel disease is one of the pain syndromes that Sarno has noticed are taking epidemic proportions in the last few decades in the United States. It is his observation there are what he calls **equivalent maladies** that occur in people who suffer from some form of inner psychic-emotional pain that is either repressed or suppressed. Some of these equivalent maladies which he attributes to TMS are fibromyalgia, sciatica, dizziness, migraine and tension headaches, frequent urination, sexual dysfunction, tinnitus, irritable bowel syndrome, gastro-esophageal reflux, and spastic colitis.

Lisa's tendonitis was related to repetitive motions at her work place, but also to the personality pattern of demanding perfection from herself and putting her needs and desires last.

Lisa expected herself to be a superwoman at home and work. She had an alcoholic husband whose behaviour often enraged her. The defensive posture of her forearms with its tension and pain symbolically represented her own defensiveness and rage. Underneath her defensiveness was a pattern of judging herself and others. Lisa had three experiences that involved chronic pain-a bicycle accident, an automobile accident and work related tendentious.

Lisa knew these experiences were messages telling her she needed to have a more balanced, less stressful life-style. Clues to the messages of her imbalance came from the location and bodily functions of her injuries, on her right side-her right forearm, and back. This seemed to indicate a driven, yang approach to life. Her pain forced her to slow down, relax and go inward to develop more spirituality. Lisa was an admitted perfectionist, with a type #1 personality, a person who wanted to reform or do things right. She was the oldest daughter in a large family in which she helped raise her younger siblings. During her mid-life crisis, Lisa faced her rage over her husband's destructive behavior and confronted him with its impact upon her.

THE HEALING OF PAIN

Pain can become an ally when it alerts us to where we need to grow and change. Pain does not go away just by venting or expressing emotions, because it is a current of energy that deadens and isolates us. Healing pain has to involve not just focusing upon the pain itself, but upon what is the source of this pain. Begin this process of exploring the present pain and seeing it as a current or flow of energy for which there is a common denominator or negative ego pattern. In doing this, recognize although we did not ask for consciously create this pain, we allow it.

To break through her pattern of pain, Lisa began to contemplate what the emotional and mental pain she needed to face. She like her mother had sacrificed her own desires and interests for others. She made a list of all the areas of her life in which she felt stressed and angry. The most conflicted area of her life was her relationship with her alcoholic husband and her despair over their deteriorating relationship.

Lisa began asking for the changes she desired. As part of her mid-life crises, she decided to pay attention and act upon those interests for which she held genuine passion. The people who depended upon her for their comfort and income discouraged her from following her passions. Lisa realized it was her pattern always to please others and put herself last like her mother did. She decided to change by following her creative impulses by becoming more mindful.

Mindfulness is a positive part of the Buddhist religious tradition that teaches how we can minimize suffering in our lives by being more aware of our thoughts and feelings and by choosing to change the ones that foster pain. Mindfulness is a practice of meditation in which a person observes their thoughts and feelings without judgement with the purpose of eliminating as much suffering as possible. The purpose of this practice is to alleviate suffering and improve health and spirituality. Mindfulness can be particularly helpful for people who suffer from physical pain by helping them to avoid the repression or suppression of angry or fearful thoughts and feelings.

However, our negative ego patterns often hardwire us to suffering by triggering the old negative ego patterns that once served to protect us as children. These patterns of emotion activate the fight and flight responses which result in automatic fear or anger responses. We can change these automatic responses through a process or mindfulness in which we consciously observe the arousal of old patterns and then choose more positive ones. Lisa's automatic reaction was to be a perfectionist who considered everyone else's interests and approval before her own desires.

When her stress reactions occurred, she learned to stop and reflect and ask herself, "What other options do I have besides this old fearful one?" The steps in this mindful approach are **to Stop, Breathe, Recognize, Own, Forgive and Choose** to respond in more healthy, positive ways. On the physical level this choice by-passed the action of the amygdala, the alarm system of the lower brain. When this alarm system is triggered, it alerts the body to prepare to meet the perceived danger. Among other things, our heart rate and blood pressure go up. Muscle tension increases and hormones such as adrenaline and cortisol are secreted into the blood stream. At the same time our digestive, immune, reproductive systems and other process that support our vitality and health are suppressed. Essentially this alarm system puts us into a defensive mode geared up to meet danger.

Even when stress reactions have been triggered, the individual can override these by choosing to pay attention to more positive options. This individual can pause to reflect on how an old negative ego pattern has been triggered and then can choose to replace it with courage, appreciation, love, caring and gratitude. These more positive thoughts and feelings serve as an antidote to lower level automatic fear reactions.

To begin a healing process, the key is to focus upon being aware of the constrictive feelings held in your body and the affect these had upon you. Then you can begin to release these constrictive feeling through the breath. In the process of deep breathing, you then reflect upon your pattern of behavior, and make other more healthy choices.

A negative ego pattern is healed if we have no emotional baggage from it and can quickly shift to a more positive

perspective if and when it does temporarily return. We can get stuck in any one of the steps of processing a painful illness. We can refuse to recognize, own, forgive or heal an illness. Most often in our society, we do not realize that recognizing and owning our responsibility for our part in creating an illness. Our resistance to awareness stops us from having power over what needs to be healed. With this resistance to awareness, we give up the power to heal it, not just remove our symptoms. We give that power over to health professionals who sometimes wish to be helpful but lack the methods or means to help us.

It is important to realize that we are the final authorities over our bodies and if we lack the will to live or are not willing to do our part in healing ourselves, we cannot blame others for being unable to help us get well. Forgiving ourselves for our past mistakes is essential if we want to transcend the physical environment that weakened our bodies. The simple step of admitting that we need spiritual help to lift certain negative ego patterns can be critical in the healing of an illness. Help is always there if we are humble enough to ask for it. This act of course must be followed by a willingness to change the toxic environment that helped produce the illness in the first place.

Bill was a workaholic whose health rapidly deteriorated as soon as he left his position as a bank president. This work position was what had bolstered his self esteem and gave him the most pleasure and esteem. Bill was a divorced man whose relationships with the women in his life were shallow and conflicted. He truthfully did not know how to relate to women as equals. During retirement he tried to return to the male centered activities of his life, his interest in sports and gambling. He never fully trusted his feminine side and when he began experiencing sciatic pain in his back and legs instead of trusting his own inner guidance, he allowed himself to undergo several botched surgeries on his back that left him in continual pain.

Bill had never learned to be introspective and was frightened and resistant to even looking into the real source of his pain. As an adolescent, he had experienced a number of painful beatings from his father in the same area of his body that now was so painful. He had buried this pain and denied that these early experiences had any relationship to the pain he now felt. Some of his spirit had been lost in those painful experiences. Bill was able to heal some of his pain by writing his feelings in poetry and a journal. Through journaling, Bill began to open up to feelings he had long suppressed and repressed concerning his relationship with his father and his distrust of the feminine in his life.

Part of his healing was to connect that free adolescent he was to let him know he needed the spirit of freedom he then had to give him back his will to live again. In meditation, he asked this adolescent to join him. He let him know they could give back the shame and pain back to his father who had given it to him through his frequent physical beatings. He did this by recalling the pain he felt and through imagery giving it back to his father. The adolescent he once was had a free courageous spirit that he now needed to get back the sense of value he had lost when he retired. He needed to feel the value of vitality and enthusiasm the young adolescent part of himself could again give him.

WRITING DOWN OUR PAIN FOR
BETTER HEALTH AND HEALING

One of the most efficient, elegant ways to heal our pain and the painful stories it symbolizes is through writing in a soulful expressive way. Unexpressed traumas tend to keep us stuck in old patterns of behavior. However expression alone is not enough unless it leads to thinking, insight, reflection and resolution and release of old negative ego patterns. The research of James Pennebaker, a psychologist at the University of Texas supports the relationship between unexpressed traumas and illness. In 1984, Pennebaker surveyed 200 people from the Dallas area. He was surprised to find that of those surveyed; the 65 people who had traumas they never confided to others were the ones who suffered from all kinds of illnesses including ulcers, cancer, heart disease and the flu.

Pennebaker then tested the mental, emotional and physical effects of different kinds of disclosure of a trauma upon three groups of college students. He asked each of the three groups to write for ten minutes a day for four days. The first group was told to write in an open, meaningful way their thoughts and feelings concerning a traumatic experience. The second group was asked to write only a detailed description of what happened in this traumatic experience. The third group was to write only about their feelings concerning a traumatic incident. The first group was the only one that benefited from their disclosure by having lower blood pressure, higher immune functioning and better health for six weeks afterwards.

The implications of open, soulful disclosure through language are immense to the prevention and healing of illness. Writing involves all of the senses and is a way to balance the left brain use of language with the right brain tendencies to negativity. Pennebaker's associates did a word analysis of the first group of student writing and discovered that the quality of writing for these students moved not only to release of emotion but to a resolution of their experiences. These students had stories with a beginning, middle and an ending reflecting the happy ending of their better health.

SHADOW WORK-CHAPTER THREE-
HEALING THE PAIN

1. Honestly assess those places in your present life where you suffer. Breathe into those places and fill them with love and hope. Define how you wish these to heal.

2. How is this pain and suffering an ally which alerts you to where you need to grow and change?

3. Write out your painful story and identify its core beliefs and feelings. Then ask, "What is the theme of this story?" What did you lose of your health, energy, creativity, or love as a result of this story? Write another story to replace it that has a healthier, happier ending. Reward yourself for writing this new story.

4. What religious, cultural or familial beliefs contribute to your pain?

5. How is the stress in your life a shadow of pain? What is the source of the fear beneath this stress? Is it a loss of power, a need to belong, or another need such as the need to be creative or experience your spirituality?

6. What does your negative ego say about why you need to struggle and suffer? While experiencing your negative ego pattern being triggered, take the steps mentioned in the text by first noticing your stress reaction, breathe deeply, let go of your negative thoughts and feelings, forgive yourself and refocus your mind.

Chapter Four

Healing Our Collective Dark Shadows

*H*ealing ourselves requires that we take back our power from collective beliefs that have denied it. These beliefs tell us we are the victims of our bodies and have no power to heal ourselves. The official line of consciousness believes we live in a world that is unsafe or untrustworthy, nor can we trust ourselves or our goodness, so we think we must defend ourselves from what is outside and within us. The collective belief that illness is purely a physical matter denies the powerful interaction of body and mind and our natural abilities to heal ourselves and others.

Recognizing the Shadow Beliefs Common in our Society

The consequences of shadow work are personal, but the affect upon our world and humanity is monumental. If we devote ourselves to this official line of consciousness, the world will always appear to be a fearful place. However, we can gradually move away from this official line of consciousness by questioning our personal beliefs and their consequences. You can begin to say, "I live in a safe universe," and as a result you will. These are some of the unhealthy beliefs which cause us to be more defensive and thus more stressed: *I am not important. I am powerless. I am unworthy. I have to be perfect to please people. Mistakes or failures are bad. Change is difficult and takes a long time. I am not good enough. I am stupid. I am incapable. Nothing I do is good enough or important. What makes me good enough or important is pleasing other people. I will never get what I truly want. If I make mistakes or fail, I will be abandoned and rejected.* As an adult, we can gradually focus on more positive feelings and beliefs that support our safety and confidence and our defenses will no longer be needed, as we will no longer attract stressful and threatening experiences.

Each of these unhealthy beliefs is acquired by us as children to make sense of the events around us. This does not mean we need to blame our parents for their less than optimal child raising practices because most parents have never been taught how to be good parents, and are not aware of the impact of their words or actions upon their children. There is a constant conflict between parents wanting their children to be quiet, neat and to do what they are told and what children by nature are capable of being.

As a young child of three or four years of age, my parents had little time to spend with me because they owned a small family grocery store during the depression. Both of my parents were Swedish immigrants who were struggling to learn English. My father Torston Holmstrom was very ill during this time with an enlarged heart condition and did not have much time or strength to pay attention to both me and the state of his business and health. My father died when I was only three years old, and my mother hired an elderly housekeeper to help care for me and my sister.

Although we think we observe the meaning or our interpretation of these childhood events, our interpretation is only one of many possible interpretations. Since most parents are not skilled in raising children, it is unproductive to blame our parents as they often did not know how to parent well. We look at their behaviour and try to make sense of their behavior. In my case, I concluded, "I am not important." My parents were both good people who did the best they knew how to raise my sister and I. Meanwhile, I as a child interpreted their lack of attention to mean. "I am unimportant." This belief became part of my subconscious. Another closely related belief also came from my interpretation of their behavior. This belief was, "What I have to say is not important." As an adult, I had to first acknowledge that these unhealthy beliefs were indeed true for me, so I could change them. These beliefs were also the source of my chronic throat and expression problems with cysts in my neck as a teenager, hypothyroidism with a goiter at my throat in my mid-years and perennial stage fright whenever I had to give a speech before an audience.

We can use our bodies as a monitor as to whether any of these statements are true or not for us. One way to do this is through saying these statements out loud and seeing whether or not we have a gut feeling about whether or not a statement is true for us. We can intellectually dismiss a statement, but our bodies know on a subconscious level whether or not it is true for us. A belief is either true or it is not; it is never partially true.

To be aware of how unhealthy this shadow is we first must pause, relax and ask ourselves some fundamental questions. These basic questions are these: What was happening when I was a young child that caused me to interpret my parent's behavior in the way I did? In my case my belief: "*I was unimportant,*" was only one interpretation, not what was actually true.

This dark law helped me give meaning to events I did not understand at the time, but there were many other possible interpretations of those events which would be much healthier for me. These more healthy interpretations would have been to visualize these events as a video and have some wise person suggest other interpretations such as: (1) My parents were preoccupied with their survival and unaware of my needs. (2) They may have been too busy to tell me that I was already good enough to begin with and important and did not need to say or do anything to prove this. (3) Another interpretation is that even if my parents did not see me as important at the time, they were wrong.

These new interpretations need to be focused upon to replace the dark law that placed me in a defensive, constrictive position that can be the source of illness later on in my life. Our bodies share with our subconscious minds the primary need to make us safe and to promote our survival. If we are to grow, we need to consciously let our subconscious minds know that old constrictive programs no longer work for us, and we choose to replace them with healthier ones.

OUR COLLECTIVE DARK SHADOW

To let our collective shadows die, we first need to be aware of how they oppress us and how this shadow leaves us with less imagination, compassion, dreams and wisdom The old conventional life-style can be replaced by a new one that is not only more healthy and less stressful, but more expansive, creative, happier and truer. Marie-Louise von Franz, a Jungian Analyst and associate of Jung, in the documentary film about Jung's life called "A Matter of Heart," speaks about the evil which occurred in Nazi Germany when the personal shadows of individuals coalesced with the collective, evil shadow of the Nazis. The personal shadows of individual Germans of greed and jealousy for the Jews became a bridge to the Nazi movement whose evil was demonic. Under this cultural shadow, individual Germans acted in ways more evil than they would have acted alone. Marie-Louise von Franz used the analogy of a house in which one door is open through which evil can enter.

If each of us is aware of our shadow door, our inferior qualities, or the ways in which we could be seduced to evil, we can keep that door shut. I know, for instance, I could be controlling to my clients or family members, but since I know the darkness, and the potential evil of this door, I keep it shut. I have also become aware that when I abandon myself by believing I am insignificant and do not matter, the path of my enneagram disintegration as a peacemaker, I am aware of the door to the dark shadow that devalues not only myself, but the elderly and women. The rejection of this collective shadow allows room for me to nurture my talents, and the relationship with the Creator I desire. My spirituality and creativity then comes alive and I become my truer, more whole self.

FINDING BALANCE IN AN IMBALANCED SOCIETY

When feminine energy is denied, what is also denied is the possibility that any of us, either male or female, can experience and receive the special unconditional love and co-creation of the feminine side of human life that depends upon the use of our imagination in a powerful way. To open to this feminine experience in and around us, we need to examine the cultural beliefs that blind us to it.

These are some questions that can help us be more aware of the unnecessary stressful, imbalanced life-styles that can foster illness:

(1) To what extent does my demand for logic, reason, and perfection kill or deny my imagination and creativity? How does this demand prevent me from imagining myself as more healthy?

(2) How does the nobility of structure and order deny my spirituality and the dignity of the beautiful chaos in my life?

(3) Am I so bound and tied down by duty and obligation that I can no longer feel desire or experience passion?

(4) Are appearance and performance so important to me that I have no room for soul and spirit?

(5) Is the hierarchy and demands for competition and comparison so important to me that I am blinded to the hierarchy of support and love that is available to me?

(6) Is the value of struggle and the need to be valued as a product of social profitability so important to me that I have shut out the spiritual forces that can help me co-create?

The powerful, magical way of co-creation has become less and less known in our western culture. A living imagination has been denied because it is associated with the feminine. It is not only women who have been ignored, denied and been made invisible, but the feminine energy in men as well. The feminine energy suffers in both women and men. Without a living imagination, men cannot find their true masculinity, nor can women fulfill their true femininity.

The Holy Grail is an ancient myth that speaks of the power of feminine energy to help us heal ourselves and others. This myth speaks of the denial of the Goddess energy of imagination, desire and conception; if we deny, reject and refuse to incorporate this energy within ourselves, we are sterile and stagnant both as individuals and as a society.

In the Grail legend, King Amfortas is sick and wounded by his shadow, a pagan warrior. Just as the king is wounded and infertile so has his whole kingdom become a waste land. Everybody is living an inauthentic life, doing what they are told to do with no courage to be true to themselves. In the Grail legend, young Perceval has been brought up in the country close to nature by a mother who taught him to revere nature and to trust his intuition and inner guidance. However, when he became an adolescent his father wished him to be trained as a knight. This training required him to give up his natural curiosity and compassion and to follow orders rather than his own impulses.

When Perceval comes to the Grail Castle to meet the wounded grail King, he does not inquire about his uncle's health. He had the impulse to ask his uncle, "What is amiss?" but he refrains from expressing his compassion because his training as a knight does not allow for this kind of concern. The grail king is unable to get well by himself for he does not trust himself to inquire into the real cause of his illness. Since he will not engage with his illness and recognize its source, he cannot heal. Every mythical hero who wishes to be healed and a healer must face his own shadow side to be of help to others.

It is the shadow that contains illness, but the encounter with the shadow that brings us to a new place of consciousness where what is missing can be recognized and healed. When Perceval returns for a second time after descending into his own dark shadow side, he is mature enough to be compassionate and to trust himself enough to inquire of his uncle, "What is amiss?"

The healing of an individual and collective patterns of belief come not by following the rational rules represented by the rigid knights of armor, but the natural opening of the heart in love and compassion for the suffering of another human being. To be authentic, an individual has to reject the chauvinist expectations of a society that go against his or her own authentic truth.

The pagan shadow that wounds the King lives a life close to nature, a life that does not separate matter from spirit, or mind from body. It is the impulses from nature that give life its authenticity, not the rules coming from an outside, human authority. This is the truth that lies within the Grail legend. The grail becomes symbolic of an authentic life lived according to its own will and unique impulses; this integrity carries an individual between the opposites of light and dark, good and evil.

Balancing through Centering
and Detachment

It is paradox that the only way we can come to a place of detachment is to be at first vulnerable and intensely involved in expressing our emotional responses within the situations we encounter. Sometimes it is appropriate to express our emotions; sometimes it is not. If we express our anger at a boss we could lose a job for instance. If we suppress our emotions often, there is a cost. Suppression extends the effects of stress and intensifies an emotion. The suppression of anger for instance may be the source of many illnesses and physical symptoms such as head and back aches.

The clean balanced way of communication that fosters good health is the detached, wise way. Detachment does not imply uncaring or lack of involvement. On the contrary, detachment is a function of intensity. A person who has intensity is in the moment, and lets go of the moment when it is finished. The intensity of detachment means being involved with our hearts, our minds, and in our bodies. Only when we are willing to be intensely with an emotion or situation can we find detachment from it. If we refuse to experience an emotion or situation intensely, we are attached to it, no matter how adroitly we may deny, suppress, or avoid it. Detachment means that we not only experience intensely but that we appropriately deal with the impact of this experience with honesty and wisdom.

If we are emotionally detached, the anger or hurt we experience can be like a ball that comes at us. We can catch, feel, and then let go of it, or we can allow it to hit us on the head and injure us. When we refuse to deal with our experiences and feelings, as they occur, allowing them to hit us, then we carry them for years, letting them have the power to give us illnesses such as diabetes or brain cancer years later. `By experiencing an emotion fully in the moment, we use its energy to fuel us and not the possible negativity that could grow from it.

When we suppress, avoid, or deny our emotions in the name of a twisted sense of nobility or detachment, we are providing an external source of fuel to that very energy we pretend does not affect us. The balanced way of detachment is healthy, because no emotions are suppressed, denied, or stuffed in our bodies or subconscious or unconscious minds. Then we are free of their possible, unhealthy affects upon us.

To know what your physical symptoms symbolize, you can go in meditation directly to your physical symptoms and ask what feelings are hidden there. It is important to focus upon how you respond to whatever feelings such as guilt, fear, or anger are hidden there. Do you shrink, cower, go into self-pity, blame, become a martyr, go into bravado or become curious? Engage this negative ego pattern by making it an image or object that you can step beyond. You do this by giving that feeling a shape, color, or texture that your soul and higher self can help you erode or dissolve.

From a place beyond this feeling, you turn back and look at it. What you are doing is objectifying your feeling and giving your unconscious and subconscious the message that you are making these feelings objects that you place outside yourself. You then step into a future place of health beyond whatever feeling such as anger, fear, or guilt that you have been hiding both in your unconscious and body.

WHO ARE WE REALLY?

We are spiritual beings having a physical experience, but to truly understand this experience we are subject to all of the rules that affect our physical bodies. We are more than our bodies. Many people have experiences in which they left their bodies for short periods of time and survived without them. Psychic tell us we often leave our bodies when we dream. We have many death experiences during our lives. We do not have the same bodies we had when we were children, adolescents or young adults. Nor do we have the same thoughts, feelings, or beliefs.

We form beliefs to give meaning to events that have many possible meanings. Then we see the meaning we choose to have out in the world. Each of us is a belief creator who as a child created beliefs by interpreting the behavior of our parents. Our bodies are like the unformed clay that we mold and sculpt with our beliefs and their related feelings. There was a part of us that created meaning from our experiences by creating beliefs to explain those experiences. We did this to survive and feel safe as children even if those beliefs were untrue and later constricted our growth.

Since we were the ones who created our beliefs, we are also the ones who can change them. We can reassess our reality and decide what beliefs would be healthier and less stressful. We can ask ourselves questions such as, "What is missing to allow me to be more powerful, healthy, whole, satisfied, or successful?" "What is possible for me now?"

We can eliminate all beliefs that cause us problems and with these the feelings associated with those beliefs. My belief for instance that what I said or wrote was not important lead me to feel futile and depressed. By replacing it with a truer belief that I have a positive impact through my words and writing, allowed me to feel more enthusiastic and fulfilled. We are different than other animals in our ability to discern the meaning behind our experiences and to give those experiences a truer meaning.

THE UNHEALTHY CONSEQUENCES OF
PERFECTIONISM AND STRUGGLE

Della, who I wrote of earlier in chapter one, by most standards, would be considered a successful career woman who was literally "burned out" at what she felt were the impossible demands of her work. A demand for perfection is both a personal and collective dark shadow. It is a personal demand as well also a cultural one. Della was an admitted perfectionist who learned to get ahead by performing perfectly to whatever standards her employers, teachers or family set for her. She explored what the inner symbolism of her illness might be. The physical symptoms were overweight, troublesome menstruations and cystitis of her sexual organs. Della believed this unhealthy core belief: *What makes me good enough or important is doing things perfectly.*

Cystitis is an inflammation involving conflicts in the pleasure-creativity chakra areas. The inflammation of the sexual area of her body complemented the shadow of her inflamed, burned out attitude at work. She found no pleasure in her work and was too exhausted and anxious to be creative at home. Her pattern of perfectionism was unhealthy because it caused her to be chronically anxious. Under this anxiety was a fear she would make a mistake. Della could never allow herself to make a mistake, because this meant she was a failure.

To heal her pattern of shame and perfectionism, I asked Della to work with her subconscious contract with her father. She believed her father expected her to be superhuman. To protect and survive her childhood, Della had contracted with her father to be perfect according to his rules. Even though she no longer had to deal with her father, she still had his standards in her psyche as the command of her negative ego self, "Be Perfect," or something dire would happen. She feared that she would lose her job as her job performance had been less than perfect. As a result, she was experiencing acute inner stress. By writing out her shame contract with her father over a period of three days and destroying it, Della was able to clear her subconscious mind of some of the shame-based beliefs of her childhood.

The subconscious has the function of selecting and protecting us from too much information by bringing to conscious awareness only that which is consistent with our beliefs. To understand the subconscious, it is helpful to see it as a place that can be described. Most often the subconscious is seen as a labyrinth, a huge library, a large storage place, the Hades an underworld or a high tech control room.

We discussed some of the common fears about working with the subconscious. One of these is the fear that we may have to face all the ugly beliefs, motivations and feelings that we resist seeing. It was uncomfortable and sad for Della at first to realize her perfectionist standards of behaviour were aggravating her stress. I explained to Della by identifying where her fear came from-parents, school, metaphysics or religion, or psychology, she could overcome and cut this fear short.

I encouraged her to work with her subconscious to become healthier. I explained that since her subconscious stored her emotions, to the extent she feared the intensity of them she might also fear her subconscious. The subconscious merely held these emotions, but is not these emotions; it did hold Della's belief she had to be perfect to please those who she felt controlled her survival and safety.

The Inner Stress of Perfectionism

Perfectionists are found at all socioeconomic levels. The personality drive most associated with perfectionism is that of trying to do the right thing. The error of the perfectionist is to look to an outside measure of perfection for his or her direction rather than to the unique pattern of his or her true self. If you are a perfectionist, you will always feel like a failure and therefore always be anxious. The yardstick of perfection by which you measure yourself will place impossible demands upon you. These impossible demands are sources of inner stress. It is the negative ego, the enemy of the shadow, who tells us, "Be perfect."

This negative ego has, as its goal, an impossible idealized self rather then the genuine self which is the ideal of your shadow. The negative ego tells you the lie, "You are better or less than others." The shadow encourages you to be true to your own creative impulses and integrity. The unhealthy pattern of perfectionism leads to undue anxiety and stress common in autoimmune illnesses such as cancer.

This negative yardstick can also be expressed in avoiding or procrastinating in situations in which performance will be judged. It can also be expressed in overcompensation in which one does not care about standards at all. Thus creative tasks are done without attention to standards in a hasty, careless manner assuring failure. Anxiety is always present when there is perfectionism because these standards are unrealistic and uncreative.

If you are perfectionist, it is unlikely you will be creative. When you do not allow yourself to venture to do and be free to make mistakes, or try new ways of doing things, it is impossible to create. Rigid standards of perfectionism are stressful because they prevent you from thinking outside the box, and from being free and spontaneous.

HEALING UNHEALTHY FAMILY BELIEFS AND PATTERNS

Many mind/body interactions that are ignored and go undiagnosed in America are considered stress related disorders in other countries. These disorders are related to family and cultural beliefs that are unhealthy and unduly stressful. Japan has defined twenty conditions as psychosomatic. One of these is "autonomic nervous system imbalance," a disorder not officially recognized in the United States, but one that Dr. Andrew Weil has observed in people who have cold hands in warm rooms.

Those who display this disorder have reduced circulation to the hands when they have an overactive sympathetic nervous system which causes digestive problems and the small arteries in the extremities to constrict. Dr. Weil treats this disorder by mind/body approaches rather than drugs. Jake, a young man, displayed this disorder with cold hands in a warm room. He told me how he numbed his feelings of fear and anger by denying them and using drugs.

Jake was surprised when I said, "Just because you deny your feelings doesn't mean they go away. Your fears go right into your body and give you cold hands and feet." I explained that when we are afraid, blood flows away from our hands and feet into the core of our bodies to help us survive an attack from the dangers within or outside us. We then explored what his other life stresses were. Jake was failing two classes in his senior year of high school and was in danger of not graduating.

Jake was also the youngest member of a dysfunctional family in which his father was an alcoholic, and he was the caretaker of a co-dependent mother. Jake saw his role in the family as keeping his mother happy and protecting her from the anger of his father. Jake had the automatic emotional pattern of getting angry whenever he was afraid to keep people whom he feared away. Jake had learned this pattern from his father who used it to frighten the other members of his family into submission to his needs. One of the lessons Jake needed to learn was he was not responsible for the feelings of his parents or whether or not there was peace in the relationship between his parents.

To heal this imbalanced reaction, Jake had to give his body different orders and have a more trusting, accepting picture of the world and his place in it. Each of our minds is like a government official who directs the citizen cells of our bodies. If our minds have paranoid beliefs that tell our cells to mobilize for defensive action, to pare down other activities such as digesting or circulating blood to our extremities, then these energies do not function well. The body in response to the mind's perceived threats in the world may develop an autoimmune disease or an imbalanced nervous disorder.

The stressful life-style of many people in our western world involves anxiety and an unduly defensive reaction. Anxiety is undefined anger, fear, loneliness, jealousy and despair. Whatever we focus upon we draw to us. Jake was a talented basketball player who had learned to refocus his attention when he was not playing well. With this change of focus, and a more trusting, positive attitude to himself, his playing improved.

Anxiety and depression eventually take a toll upon the body; these unresolved feelings are dangerous inner stressors that can cause the immune system and our major organs to malfunction. We can consciously heal ourselves by changing our beliefs, their related feelings, and the focus of our attention. Just as Jake changed his focus and resonance during his basketball game to go on to perform better, we can refocus our fearful thoughts and feelings to clear our blockages of thought and feeling. Jakes' fear was an aspect of his negative ego pattern and a shame-based contract with his parents to protect his mother from his father and other people she feared.

CONFRONTING AND TRANSFORMING OUR NEGATIVE EGOS

The body as a reflection of our shadow and subconscious mind and feelings always tells the truth. The negative ego, on the other hand, lies to us. It tells us we are separate with no connection or help from the universe; it judges and separates and thus isolates us from spirituality and others. It tells us we are insignificant, helpless, and hopelessness in an unfriendly universe. The negative ego, in harbouring feelings of anger and fear and their related beliefs, can threaten our health.

A healthy ego carries messages to us from our environment. It is not supposed to have the power to make decisions or choices. An ego becomes negative when instead of doing its job of giving messages to the self, it is asked to make decisions or choices. Then it has to run old negative patterns from our childhood or the past based on old thoughts and beliefs. It is important to be conscious of its repetitive patterns, so we do not identify with them. When we become aware of the presence of these patterns, we can pause, reflect and choose not to act upon them.

Our negative egos are weak and can make us ill because they represent a lesser part of ourselves. Some of the destructive lies the negative ego tells you are, "You must always struggle to be valuable," "Be perfect." "Don't feel, especially anger or people will never love you." "Just do what others approve of and you will be loved." "Unless you are succeeding at every endeavour, you are a failure." The meanings we give to events most often began in our childhoods when we formed beliefs about us and life that ultimately determine what we do and feel. Since we each created our beliefs, we can change our lives by changing the beliefs that are part of our negative ego. The way we can change these beliefs is a process of transforming our negative egos. This process can be done either in an altered state in meditation or through dialoguing and writing questions and listening to the repetitive voices in a more alert conscious state:

(1) **Begin by asking our spiritual sources to protect us from our own negative egos.** To do this we can use images of a protective cloak, shield or ball of light. When

you first encounter your negative egos, remember it is not your friend and it is a weak lesser part of yourself which you need not fear.

(2) **Ask for an image of this ego to appear.** Allow it to enter and notice whether it is male or female and how threatening it is to you.

(3) **Let it tell you what its agenda is for you.** Listen to its complaints, and what its negative agenda is. If it comes as an objector-protector, tell it why you no longer need this kind of protection. Thank it for its past protection, but let it know you choose to take care of yourself.

(4) **Respond with compassion, but with authority.** Tell it why its program of negativity is not acceptable to you. If it tells you not to risk mistakes, you need to be strong and courageous enough to be wrong in the pursuit of what is right.

(5) **Visualize the energy as light or force around your negative ego diminishing.**

(6) **Imagine yourself standing where it stood and absorbing some of the energy it stole from you back into yourself.**

(7) **Then imagine what your life is like with a positive ego. Imagine the weak negative ego shifting and transforming into a positive one.**

THE DARK SHADOWS OF RELIGIOUS BELIEFS THAT FOSTER TOXIC GUILT AND SHAME

The shadow is the enemy of an idealized, inauthentic self. Some people with traditional religious beliefs deny or devalue the body especially physical functions, such as sexuality, aggressiveness, assertiveness in their drive to become a perfect spiritual human. Many religious beliefs we take for granted place unnecessary stress upon the body. The belief that each of us is inherently sinful, evil or guilty, just because we have a body is unhealthy, because it fosters attitudes of toxic shame which reject and deny the value and beauty of the human body.

This unhealthy attitude often encouraged by some forms of Christianity is the belief that by the mere fact that we are alive and have a body that we are therefore guilty and sinful. The problem with guilt is it is used as a false substitute for conscience and as a means to purify the self in an inauthentic way. The harm that guilt does is it leads to a stagnant life that blocks creativity and joy. These are some concrete steps to release, transform and heal the negative ego patterns that hold guilt in place:

SEVEN STEPS TO RELEASE GUILT

(1) **Understand what guilt is for you.** Is it disguised or denied anger? Is guilt a way to control yourself or other? Or is it a way to purify or discipline yourself? Or is guilt a way to avoiding responsibility or intimacy in relationships? Or do you use guilt as a way to justify self control or ego control? Is your guilt a sign of an imbalance of your feminine and masculine energies?

(2) **Realize that guilt is not innocent, benign, uncontrollable or noble. Guilt is anger you do not think you have a right to feel.** It is paralyzing, vicious, mean and if intense enough can be the source of illness.

(3) **Realize your inner child or adolescent may feel tremendous guilt. Work with your inner child and adolescent to**

recognize what their guilt is, so your inner child and you both understand what guilt is for you and why you feel guilty

(4) **Look for the payoffs for feeling guilty.** What specific payoffs are you getting that are more valuable to you than being free from guilt?

   a) What am I avoiding? What responsibility?
   b) Who besides me am I punishing? Who am I controlling?
   c) Who would I be betraying or less loyal to if I were less guilty?
   d) What is the feeling I am protecting? Is there any righteous anger?
   e) What does my negative ego want before I give up this guilt? What better than's, hide outs or control patterns does it want me to keep?
   f) What am I afraid to lose if I give up guilt? What self importance, what imbalance of feminine and masculine energy?

(5) **Convert the guilt into anger. Process and Release you anger**. Guilt is a cover for anger. Identify what you are angry about and release it.

(6) **Develop character, ideals and principles to replace your guilt**. After guilt is released there is a void that needs to be filled if you want to transcend its patterns. **Ideals** are those things you seek that are intangible and abstract that you are seeking such as love and peace. **Principles** are the positive boundaries you will not cross because of your ideals such as honesty, responsibility or integrity. **Character** is whether or not you adhere to your principles.

(7) Imagine specifically what your life is like when you do not feel guilty.

An attitude of guilt hides anger and encourages a denial of the body and the underlying belief that we are inherently guilty. This attitude assumes we must justify our existence by proving we are valuable and worthy. No such demand is required of us by any genuine spiritual force; a true spirituality is always based on unconditional love and forgiveness. If we feel this kind of guilt it is necessary to process it by realizing that under it is anger toward God that needs to be expressed and released.

It is impossible to forgive and accept the dark shadow of ourselves if we do not feel genuine remorse. Remorse is feeling genuine sorrow for the negative impact we do make when we make mistakes, harm others or fail. Remorse is essential to self-acceptance and is based upon the realizations that we can make mistakes and be forgiven. We are all forgivable and can be forgiven. Every child needs to learn how to feel remorse, a nontoxic form of shame, which is part of a healthy foundation of growth and change. Unfortunately many children were taught toxic shame instead.

Toxic shame is the belief that you are inherently flawed so you have to be perfect and cannot make mistakes. When we do make mistakes, this belief leads us to feeling there is something wrong or shameful in us. Shame develops in childhood when someone, usually a parent, projects their shame upon a child. The child or adolescent then believes he or she cannot make mistakes, be forgiven, or have needs and desires of their own. These beliefs are based upon a sense of separation and are motivated from a stagnant place. Toxic shame leads to self-punishment, self-effacement, and low self-acceptance.

If we cannot accept and love something within ourselves, we will find it impossible to love or accept it in others. If a woman denies her inner masculine energies, she will also deny them in men. She will reject both her inner and the outer males in her life. Similarly, the man who rejects his feminine energy will find this energy is hostile to him, both from within, and from the women in his life. To heal this conflict we need to first become aware and then accept that this shadow part of ourselves cannot be denied. If we repress our emotions and do not express them honestly and appropriately, others within our family may act them out.

In our Christian culture those things we deny, repress and reject are often those energies that arise within our human bodies naturally such as sexuality, wildness, spontaneity, anger, freedom or creativity. These are the very energies that can be expressed in honest appropriate ways to heal us and to become healthier. The feminine energies of imagination, conception and intuition may be just what not only can heal us but give us healthier religious or spiritual experiences. The unhealthy belief that we are inherently sinful and our bodies are soiled is often the source of a projection of our dark shadow upon our bodies. There is also much confusion between self love, the love we give to ourselves, and being selfish. Some religious practices discourage self love because self-sacrificing practices benefit a religious institution or cause.

There is a huge difference between spirituality and traditional religion. Many religious practices and beliefs are neither spiritual, nor moral. Spirituality is our relationship with God/Goddess/All There Is. This relationship is unique to each of us. We can learn much from the wisdom in all of religious traditions and reject those that are chauvinist and unwise. To heal imbalanced spiritual beliefs, it is necessary to remember to honor the body as made of soul substance and spirit energy.

SHADOW WORK CHAPTER FOUR-HEALING OUR COLLECTIVE DARK SHADOWS

1. What family or cultural patterns have been detrimental to your health?

2. Does the Grail Myth apply to you or your family or social group?

3. How important are the values of competition, performance and comparison to your family or social group? Are your personal values balanced?

4. Can you change your perspective about the outer stresses and see them as challenges within your control that fit into your sense of commitment to yourself? If not, make other choices.

5. What is your anxiety level? What fear, loneliness, anger, despair or unrecognized love lies beneath that anxiety? Process and let this go.

6. In meditation, ask for an image of your negative ego. Give it a stage to tell you what its agenda is for you. What are its unhealthy beliefs and feelings? Tell it why this agenda no longer works for you.

7. Write daily about what it is that causes you to be stuck and afraid to grow. Listen to the voice of your soul to help you find answers to help you heal.

Chapter Five

The Healing Process

THE BODY AS A MONITOR OF EMOTIONAL PATTERNS

*W*hen emotional patterns that reflect feelings of fear, hurt, shame, hopelessness and anger are placed within our shadow self and bodies for long periods of time, then denied or rejected, they become toxic and potential sources of illness. The shadow not only holds repressed emotional patterns, it also holds energies related to these patterns such as sexuality or assertiveness. To keep these energies repressed requires much energy and robs the individual of the grace and spontaneity that would be more natural to their growth and development.

When we want to know what unhealthy emotional patterns are in our subconscious minds, we need only to focus on the body, particularly the places that hold pain, disease or tension. This focus is the first step in recognizing our core destructive emotional beliefs and their related feelings. Just as any computer needs to be updated with newer, better patterns, so do our bodies and subconscious minds need to be renewed. Many of our old beliefs are based on a defensive fearful posture that helped us survive our childhoods, but are neither healthy nor based upon the higher truth of who we really are. The body is a reflection of the patterns we are running in unseen layers of our consciousness.

Eleanor Limmer M.S.W.

OUR RESISTANCE TO AWARENESS

One of the ways we can identify the shadow is by recognizing that when illness is present there is something imbalanced within our life-style that needs us to pay attention to be aware that we may be rejecting a vital part of ourselves. The woman who has repressed her sexuality for instance may have difficulty accepting her teenage daughter's sexual development. One sign of the shadow's presence is an intense dislike, criticism or neglect of various parts of our bodies.

Reclaiming our shadow selves makes us more accepting and less judgmental of ourselves and others. Negative ego patterns do not have to hijack us, if we are aware of their warning signals of fight, flight, or freeze and their cascade of physical symptoms such as shallow breathing, feeling hot or cold, rapid heart beat, muscle tension, anxiety or keyed up feelings, and changes in vocal tone. The body is letting us know through these symptoms that we need to wake up and recognize their potential dangers, so we can choose other healthier attitudes.

Emotions patterns are both thoughts and feelings. Healing always starts by focusing on the body to explore what feelings are present, and then by consciously lifting the resonance of our feelings gradually to a more expansive, healthy level. All feelings are positive as long as they are expressed honestly and appropriately. Anger in a situation of oppression is appropriate when handled honestly and can help free us from that situation by giving us the energy to act. These feelings may evoke memories of incidents from childhood when beliefs and feelings were created and stored in the subconscious to makes sense of and survive threatening parental behavior.

There are certain emotional patterns that counteract the natural activity of the seven chakra areas of the body and the functions of the organs that are in these areas. The Eastern traditions have called these patterns demons. The emotional pattern of **fear** blocks the natural functioning of the first chakra and prevents the individual from experiencing safety and security. The emotional pattern of **guilt** with its underlying anger blocks the functioning of pleasure of the second chakra. The third chakra's power is blocked by the emotional pattern of **shame**. The fourth chakra's function of love is blocked by **grief**. The fifth chakra function of speaking truth is blocked by the emotional pattern of **dishonesty**. The sixth chakra's intuition is blocked by **illusion**. The sixth chakra's spirituality is blocked by **attachment**.

Carl Jung once wrote, "One does not become enlightened by imagining figures of light, but by making the darkness conscious." There is little value to have a medical or an intuitive diagnosis of an illness from others if these patients do not have their own intuitive insights as to what unique emotional, mental and spiritual pattern contributed to the creation of their illnesses. These insights allow an individual to begin to take responsibility for changing their patterns and life-styles to healthier ones. This process begins by focusing upon and talking to the body in a loving accepting way.

Processing is the key to becoming more conscious and to healing. In processing we pause to breathe and **Recognize, Own, Forgive, and Choose** to replace a familiar negative pattern with a better, healthier one. Since the body and subconscious understand only present messages, it is necessary to imagine what you will feel like when you are well and what you will be doing and being as a healthy person. The following are the essential steps in any healing process.

PROCESSING TO HEAL
NEGATIVE EGO PATTERNS

RECOGNIZE; the early warning signs of constrictive feelings of fear, anger, guilt, shame, hurt, despair or loneliness.

STOP: and remind yourself: "I need to pay attention to this—now."

BREATHE DEEPLY: Relax with each exhale and release and let go of the constrictive feelings. Let the constrictive emotion soften with each breath.

REFLECT- How is this an old pattern from childhood? Is my reaction supported old myths or messages? What part of me is reacting in old constrictive ways?

FORGIVENESS: Forgive yourself for what ever mistakes or misconceptions you think you have made. Forgive others not for what they did, but for why they did it.

CHOOSE: What options do I have to this old reaction?

Can I change my mind about how I see myself in this situation? What is the best insight and choice about this situation? What is possible here with my new insight?

CHANGE: Imagine and remember how I am and will be without this old pattern.

HURT AS AN INNER STRESS

Many of the painful feelings are the residues of childhood abuse or neglect that can leave people with anger, shame, fear, hurt, emotional pain or sadness. These feelings can trigger a negative ego patterns during stressful events. Dana knew that there was more to her backache than just physical pain. Dana was enraged and hurt by many problems which affected her health. Dana was a 58 year old woman who suffered from back pain, hypothyroidism, and facial ticks. She also was experiencing a spiritual crisis.

To begin the process of acknowledging and owning to heal an illness, either your own or another's, is to start with the physical problem, and ask what negative feelings, unhealthy beliefs and patterns of behavior it symbolizes. To receive this message, Dana relaxed, breathed into her back pain, and asked what this pain symbolized. The message of Dana's painful back was, "I am carrying the responsibility of others and I am overwhelmed by impossible demands that are not my own."

By breathing into her pain and relaxing, this pain diminished. Related to this belief was the even deeper core belief: "What makes me good enough or important is the approval of others" This belief is unhealthy because it was based upon trying to get self esteem in a false and ineffective way. While focusing upon her neck and upper back pain Dana also recalled an incident in her childhood in which she had defended her mother from an abusive attack from her alcoholic father. These core beliefs and their related feelings were only one possible interpretation of the events of her childhood. We then explored other more healthy interpretations of these events by pretending that a wise mentor had viewed this scene and perhaps taken a video of it. Dana then considered these alternative interpretations: (1) My mother was wrong to expect me as a child to please and protect her (2) Just because I wasn't able to protect my mother does not mean I will always be unable to protect and be good enough to those I love. (3) My parents had unrealistic expectations of me as a child. (4) My parents and especially my father was a sick man who I could never please. Dana expressed anger, fear and resentment toward her spouse who she felt expected her to keep his impossible standards.

DANA'S NEGATIVE EGO PATTERN

Dana realized she had been abandoning her own needs and desires in deference to others, particularly those of her husband John. To understand why martyrdom is unhealthy, we must first define what martyrdom is and what unhealthy effects this negative ego pattern has upon the body. Lazaris defined martyrdom as feeling misunderstood, unappreciated, hopeless, helpless, burdened with difficulties too difficult to bear, saddled with problems too difficult to solve, as well as being held responsible for things you do not feel are your responsibility. As a result of this martyred pattern, Dana was angry and resentful. This anger and resentment prevented her from loving her husband. Martyrdom encourages self punishment and a denial that leads to hypocrisy and abuse of power.

The core trauma for Dana behind this pattern of shame and self-sacrifice began as the child of an alcoholic, abusive father and a crippled mother. At an early age, she had become her mother's designated assistant. She was expected to be a superhuman child who took on adult responsibilities beyond her capacity. Dana continued this pattern of behavior into her marriage, work and Catholic Religion. Self-sacrifice can lead to illness, because it is always accompanied by anger, hurt and stress. These feelings can be expressed as back pain, autoimmune disease or diseases such as diabetes or arthritis.

For Dana, the initial negative ego pattern was one in which she as a young child protected her mother from the physical abuse of her father. As a child, she felt a deep sense of powerlessness and rage that she could not do more to help her mother. Dana came to see herself as a protector and defender of the helpless and hopeless. To heal herself, Dana returned to this incident with her adult self to teach her inner child she was not responsible for protecting her mother from her father. As a child, she had indeed been powerless to protect her mother from this abuse.

In her adult life, Dana had many incidents which were versions of this same negative ego pattern in which the same theme of self-sacrifice and martyrdom played itself out through different actors. Dana needed to know she was powerful and did not need to sacrifice her own interests for others. Holistic healing unlike traditional medicine recognizes that beliefs and thought always take precedence over physical illnesses. Edgar Cayce, one of the pioneers of the holistic health movement stated this simply in his statement, "The mind is the builder. The body is the result." **The key to healing physical illnesses is processing through recognition, owning, forgiving and making healthier choices.**

Our unconscious and subconscious minds have no power of choice. To heal our bodies, we must place in our unconscious and subconscious minds the symbols and images that represent our healthy conscious choices. One principle of healing is this: **If we consciously choose to place in our unconscious minds expansive, positive beliefs to replace constrictive ones, these will succeed to heal and nurture our good health.** Healing depends upon cooperation between the unconscious and conscious minds.

HEALING THE HURT BENEATH BACK PAIN

Back problems often represent stuffed hurt. Dana was not only angry, but she was also hurt. This hurt was a wound like grief which took some time to release. In counselling sessions, Dana expressed her anger by writing anger letters to her husband and those she felt had manipulated her. It was difficult for her to face the humiliation of being manipulated by those she trusted who she felt had betrayed her. To heal her hurt, she had to forgive herself for allowing herself to be manipulated.

Hurt is a dangerous emotion not only because it can cause illness but because it also destroys relationships by eroding trust and love. Some people hold on to hurt either real or feigned because it gives them permission to control, to avoid responsibility, or to manipulate. They often confuse real hurt with other emotions such as anger, loneliness or humiliation which can accompany hurt but are different than it. Someone who always has to be right may claim they are hurt rather than admitting they are wrong. If someone is afraid of anger or loneliness, they may label these emotions hurt when they are not.

Hurt can be defined as consciously doing damage that causes pain either actively or passively from self doubt to anguish and deep distress. Whenever someone is manipulating to control another person, that person is being hurt. One of the main reasons people hold on to hurt is they do not know how to process to heal it. These are the steps:

(1) **Identify whether what you are experiencing is really hurt**. You can do this by asking yourself these questions: Was my trust and love eroded as a result? Did this rip some aspect of my self value- self-love, self-esteem, self-confidence, identity or self-worth? Did this slow my growth and evolution? Was I wounded and needed to take time to heal?

(2) **Feel the hurt fully.** Do this by setting aside 20 minutes using a clock or allowing time to feel nothing else but the pain, anguish and distress of your hurt. You could

do this by moaning, curling up, or sitting quietly and just feeling the pain. Follow this by taking 20 minutes to relax totally emotionally and physically by bathing, walking or just resting totally. Then let yourself feel the pain again fully for 10 minutes. Then feel good and let it go. Thus you detach yourself from the feelings.

(3) **Identify when you first let this hurt in?** Scan your childhood, adolescence and adulthood to locate where your pattern of weakness or vulnerability is? How does this pattern allow the hurt in? What incidents or series of incidents reoccur and are reinforced by negative beliefs? Notice how the same pattern reoccurs because of these areas of weakness.

(4) **Identify what the Cut is in your relationship with yourself.** The cut that this hurt produced was an injury to an important aspect of self. This cut could be an injury to your self-love, self-confidence, self-esteem, self-worth or to your identity as a person. Dana realized that as a result of this hurt, she felt less self-confidence in her ability to protect herself from being misused. Next time she would see this misuse coming and refuse to participate in this kind of manipulation because she knew she was capable of setting better boundaries, even for those she loved.

(5) **Heal the cut itself by identifying where it is in your emotional or physical body.** This pain will in time be reflected by pain in your physical body if it is not healed emotionally. You can do this in meditation using the imagery of light, energy, rain, sunlight, etc. to heal the place where you were injured. Dana was injured both in her back and throat. She used light to penetrate and visualize these physical places and wounds being opened, cleansed and healed.

(6) **Fortify the place that you let the hurt in.** To do this we need to work with our inner child, adolescent or the part of our adult self that allowed in the hurt. In meditation, work on self-love, esteem, confidence or identity that are weak or vulnerability. To build her confidence, Dana took time to listen to her inner guidance to tell her who is or is not trustworthy. She learned to trust herself more and not to allow others who she loved to manipulate or misuse her.

EMOTIONAL-PSYCHOLOGICAL SOURCES OF BACK PAIN

In Dr. John Sarno's book <u>Healing Back Pain: The Body-Mind Connection,</u> Dr. Sarno proposes that back pain is triggered by a mental-emotional response that distracts from the actual pain. Dr. John Sarno is a professor of Clinical Rehabilitation Medicine at the New York University School of Medicine and attending physician at the Howard A. Rusk Institute of Rehabilitation Medicine at New York University Medical Center.

Dr. Sarno has had success in healing by asking his patients to focus upon the real source of their pain. The back pain, he has discovered, merely serves as a distraction from the real pain that is psychological. Dr. Sarno says that the message of back pain is, "I do not want to feel this pain, so I create a pain in my back instead." Sarno attributes most of his success in curing what he calls TMS or the tension myositis syndrome to education and the rest to psychotherapy. Only 20% of his clients needed follow up psychotherapy.

Dr John Sarno has successfully treated about eighty percent of his patients by first making them aware that their real pain is not in their backs but in the painful patterns of their thought and feeling. Once the patient agrees to be responsible for their real mental-emotional pain, the back pain soon disappears. Dr. Sarno discovered perfectionism to be one of the predominant personality patterns of those who suffer from TMS symptoms. Another inner source of stress is what Sarno calls "goodism" or the hidden agenda of pleasing or getting approval from others as a source of self-esteem.

TMS is a syndrome that is the cause of the pain, numbness, tingling or weakness that many people feel. These symptoms cause real pain, but not from the diagnosis often given them. Dr. Sarno finds no correlation between the so called physical source and the pain experienced by his patients. This pain Sarno attributes to a mild oxygen deprivation which is harmless but can cause severe pain. Dr. Sarno asks his patients to talk to their bodies to tell them they will do it differently by taking care of their real pain which is most often repressed emotional anger and fear. Then their backs no longer have to carry their psychic pain for them. When a patient speaks to his subconscious mind, he begins to acknowledge that the source of his real pain is emotional, mental and spiritual.

It surprises many of Dr. Sarno's patients when he tells them they need to reject physical–structural explanations of their pain. He advises them to see the source of their back pain or its equivalent TMS problems in emotional-psychological causes. Dr. Sarno has an educational program that successfully cures back pain. He asks his patients to list, write out and express all the things that may be contributing to painful, threatening feelings. Through this process, their conflicts rose into awareness where they can be recognized, owned and healed. In his book ***Spontaneous Healing***, Dr. Weil tells of a patient named Ethan with back pain who although advised to have surgery sought other solutions. Dr. Sarno advised him that despite what his MRI showed the source of his pain was not in his back but in his emotional/mental issues. Ethan later resolved his relationship problems and his pain disappeared without surgery.

Eleanor Limmer M.S.W.

TRANSCENDING THE IMPRISONING, CONSTRICTIVE EMOTIONS BENEATH ILLNESS

There are three tiers of emotion. **The lowest tier** begins with despair/ or hopelessness, followed by loneliness, revenge, blame, jealousy/envy, hurt/betrayal, and fear/ anxiety. **The second transitional tier** begins with anger or resentment, pessimism, guilt/sadness, self-pity/overwhelm, worry/doubt, frustration/ confusion, and ends with boredom/impatience. **The highest tier of emotion** begins with well-being or satisfaction, optimism, thrill/enthusiasm, hope/trust, passion/compassion, happiness and ends with love. Healing occurs when we are able to at last reach a state of well-being, the lowest point on the expansive rung of emotions. Then you can begin to live a healthier life.

If you are caught in the lowest tier of emotion in despair, you can lift yourself gradually one or two emotions at a time to loneliness or revenge, by allowing yourself to feel these feelings, and think their related thoughts with intensity for a set period of time, such as twenty minutes, and then consciously lift yourself to a higher level of thought and feeling, such as blame. Blame is better than hopelessness, but you do not need to stay there long. You can then consciously lift yourself to jealousy or hurt, and higher.

Some new age practitioners advise people only to focus upon positive emotions. It is impossible emotionally to make such a quick jump for instance from fear to love. This does not mean rising to a higher emotion or tier has to take a long time. You can over a number of days raise yourself gradually to the upper tier. To make progress, honesty and intensity are essential. If you are stuck in one emotional stance such as fear, take the time to process where you are at and what it is you fear. Fear is a thought and a feeling of separation, of being threatened and put in jeopardy. As an instinctive response, fear can warn us of danger.

The Power of Conscious
Beliefs and Choices

To be healthy we must believe in our own good health. Our beliefs and suggestions to our bodies are constantly affecting them. These beliefs are the blueprint which organize the form of our bodies on an unconscious level. To change our bodies we have to change our conscious beliefs, even when these beliefs conflict with the physical evidence we are given concerning our bodies. We have the power of conscious choice to focus upon and to choose to be healthier, regardless of our present physical condition. Until we make a choice, we do not produce change and healing. Choice is focused intent and key to all growth, change, and healing.

You may decide to lose weight, but then also need to change any core beliefs that would interfere with this choice. One belief that would interfere with this choice would be a belief that you are unworthy to be attractive or it would be dangerous to be more attractive because it would bring you unwanted attention from the opposite sex. To change our bodies, we have to change our conscious beliefs, even when these go against consensus beliefs, cultural patterns, or physical evidence.

We are not cut off from our unconscious minds or bodies. The inner self depends upon the conscious mind to give it an assessment of the body's condition and the outer reality, and then forms the body in line with our conscious beliefs and choices. All choice is made in the conscious mind. The subconscious and unconscious do not make choices, though our choices may be hidden there. Our beliefs create the blueprint of our health or illness which we give in suggestions to our unconscious and subconscious minds.

The most crucial fourth step in the process of self-healing is choice. The more conscious we are of our choices, the more we can override and supersede shadow patterns. This healing process begins with recognizing, owning, forgiving, and then choosing to change. Mindfulness helps us observe without judgment. When shadow negative patterns are triggered there by events or stress, the emotional reaction of fear, anger, rage, shame or grief can be healed through conscious reflection and choice.

RESISTANCES TO FORGIVING SELF AND OTHERS

We don't consciously cause illnesses, but we do create the environment that predisposes us or allows illness to grow and take hold. Cancer for instance is not something we directly or willingly cause, but if we are attached to emotions such as anger or fear and tuck these emotional patterns away in our bodies without feeling, expressing and releasing them, we then lower our immune systems and create an environment in which cancers can grow. To detach from and heal our shadow emotions, it is necessary to bring these shadow patterns with their feelings and thoughts to awareness, to feel these feelings and recognize, own and forgive ourselves for them so we can release them. Forgiveness is a necessary step in the process of change and healing.

When we lack forgiveness of ourselves and our illness, we will instead judge and punish ourselves. Negative judgments separate us from feeling and keep the status quo alive, and therefore prevent us from fully recovering from an illness. There are many false ideas concerning what forgiveness is. These false ideas must be recognized, owned, and changed before we can truly forgive. Central to all forgiveness is compassion and focusing upon **why, not what** another person did to oppress or violate you. The reason this person did this to you may have been their own shame, low self-esteem, or they also had been violated. You need not forgive what was done to you but why it was done. Some of the false beliefs that need to be recognized and changed are these:

(1) Forgiveness is weak.
(2) Forgiveness is absolution or wiping away of a sin.
(3) Forgiveness is being shallow.
(4) Don't forgive because it is frightening and brings back old sorrows.
(5) If you forgive something you value such as anger, blame, excuses for failure, pieces of the past may die.
(6) If you forgive you fear the responsibility of peace, freedom, healing and joy.
(7) If you forgive you fear the love, intimacy and caring you may feel.

Forgiveness involves becoming self-conscious and taking responsibility for the beliefs and feelings that allowed or created a situation. Before forgiving others, it is always essential to first forgive yourself for allowing or creating the environment in which illness or abuse occurred. Many people fail to forgive because they simply do not know how to do so or have false ideas about its value. The steps to Self-forgiveness are these:

STEPS IN SELF-FORGIVENESS

(1) **Think about what needs to be forgiven** acknowledging you either caused or allowed something such as an illness to happen. Don't blame or feel guilt, but merely feel your

remorse (the sorrow, not guilt). Feel your desire to let hurt, anxiety, perfectionism, denied anger, or old grief, and resentments die.

(2) **Feel what needs to be forgiven** and what the various aspects of you have to say about this.

(3) **Determine what positive lessons** there are for you from this experience.

(4) **Do a meditation to forgive and feel genuine remorse.** Allow an image of the part of you that needs forgiveness to appear in your safe place. This may be the part of you that feels sorrowful, afraid, defensive, separate, uptight, angry, grieving, martyred or victimized to appear. Wrap this part of yourself in a comforting ball of energy and embrace and absorb its energy into yourself.

(5) **Determine what action** you don't have to do any longer. What can you stop doing or being?

(6) **Ask what you can feel** on the other side of forgiveness.

(7) **What do you think** on the other side of forgiveness?

At the end of a process of forgiveness, it is essential to take some time to allow new insights and awareness to reach you. Always take a moment to feel the light of forgiveness entering your body and mind. Also take some time to take back the power that you lost from parts of yourself or others by making a gesture to bring this power back into your body. How are you more real and positive? When you are dealing with an illness you may also need to forgive and feel gratitude for how your body has protected and healed you when you allowed it to. While working to forgive others remember you are not forgiving them for what they did or did not do, but **why** they acted in the way they did. While forgiving parents for instance it may be they never learned from their parents how to parent well.

HEALING NEGATIVE EGO AGENDAS
THROUGH POSITIVE TRUE AGENDAS

Hidden agendas are emotional patterns that are not socially acceptable, and to various degrees are inappropriate, destructive or impossible. A martyred person will not admit what the hidden benefits of the self-pity he or she receives as the result of her martyrdom. The most common hidden agendas are **control, vindication of your past, manipulation, revenge, self-pity or martyrdom, and trying to get praise and approval as a source of self-esteem.** Hidden agendas fall upon the continuum of being possible-impossible, constructive-destructive, or appropriate-inappropriate. Beneath every unhealthy destructive pattern there is a true one that is healthy and freeing.

Control, for instance, is often hidden because someone is not likely to admit, "I am trying to control you to get what I want." Controlling another is impossible, inappropriate, and destructive, but many people maintain, "It is my way or the highway," and subtly or overtly control the people around them to get them to do things the right way, which of course is their way.

The true agenda beneath control of yourself and others is to be self-reliant, independent and creative. The controlling person can discover they can be independent and self reliant without trying and failing to get people around them to do and be things they believe are impossible for them to achieve. There is a big difference between living your life with dominion (or control in) in which you respect yourself enough to insist on making your own choices and the domination of others in which there is (control over) in which your choices and those of others are not respected or are denied. Dominion fosters self-reliance and healthy autonomy; domination is unhealthy because it fosters rage, anger, resentment and depression.

Self-pity in the form of being a victim, or martyr, or simply feeling sorry for oneself is one of the hidden agendas that people use to get people to feel sorry for them. Instead of soliciting others to feel sorry for us, self-pity is used as an anaesthetic, and a hidden way to solicit pity. It is, after all, not socially acceptable for people to say to others, "What I really want from you is for you to feel sorry for me." However, this agenda is hidden when people use their misfortunes as victims or martyrs to get sympathy and attention from others.

Self-pity is often an anaesthetic to help you numb the pain but it can also be a way of getting others to give you special attention. The healing of self-pity comes with focusing upon the dignity of becoming self-determined by making those choices that reflect your true self. rather than those that numb you or get a hit of attention.

There are people whose **hidden agenda is to get revenge** upon others who have offended or abused them in the past. The true agenda beneath the hidden agenda of **revenge** is to **find a dominion over the constricting emotions of fear, anger, despair, and hopelessness**. Authority over these emotions can come when they are expressed honestly and appropriately, rather than denied or suppressed. The fear of anger beneath revenge will allow that anger to build until it explodes and destroys relationships and families if it is not expressed in an honest and appropriate way to those affected by it. The husband who withdraws from his wife because he fears her anger will eventually have to deal with the impact these emotions have upon their marriage.

You can explore to see if any of the most common hidden agendas are yours. Pay attention to recurrent feedback from others who complain you are being "pushy" or controlling to them. If you are repeatedly confronted with controlling, self-pitying or manipulative people, look at what it is within your shadow self that attracts these kinds of people. **You can learn how to deal with oppressive, controlling people with assertiveness and**

honesty without being victimised by them. Since your true agenda frees you of your dark shadow, it holds a message that can thrill you with new enthusiasm.

The healthy solution to the hidden agenda of **the disease to please**, is to learn to **love yourself** and others more by having more integrity and by getting your self-esteem from within. To do this you can practice being more honest, taking more responsibility in a spontaneous way, doing no harm to others, listening to the whispers in your life, and enjoying your life as much as possible. Refusing to take any one of these steps will prevent you from having true self-esteem.

If you find you depend upon **pleasing or getting the approval of others** as the main source of your self-esteem, recognize you pay the price of dependence upon outside validation which is exhaustion, autoimmune diseases and a totally competitive attitude to others. When loving relationships are considered too painful and are associated with humiliation, rejection and abandonment, some people instead of seeking love will seek instead to get praise and approval from others.

Hidden under the unhealthy pattern of trying to please or get approval is **the true healthy agenda of giving and receiving love.** Many people who have this agenda have become so disillusioned about what love is that they believe love is too painful to find because it is associated with childhood experiences of being hurt, humiliated, rejected or abandoned. The true agenda which can heal this false one of seeking approval and praise is to accept and receive love.

When you know how you do a hidden agenda, ask yourself why you tend to hide it even from yourself. **Manipulative people** believe they are not powerful so they use others to get the power they fear they do not have. Men who prey upon the good will of women use their manipulations to get the material things they believe they are unable to get for themselves. Their flattery and manipulations fail when these women find they have been betrayed and abandoned.

The true agenda behind manipulation is the true agenda of finding **and using real power**. Manipulative people can recognize how they trick and use power dishonestly, forgive themselves for this behavior, and choose to own and use their power in a more honest and reliable way. **The true agenda underneath manipulation which the shadow holds for us is to deal with fears and weaknesses directly so power is used in a direct and honest way.**

Anytime some one, through flattery or dishonesty, manipulates the good will of another, this manipulation is impossible, inappropriate or destructive. In time, the one who is manipulated will recognize the deception behind these actions, and learn to avoid and distrust the goodwill of this deceptive person. The senior citizen, for instance, who has been manipulated to invest in stocks in an unreliable investment company may be taken in by a manipulative broker, but in time will come to distrust and reject that same broker.

If you have the **hidden agenda of vindication of the past** by trying to do something spectacular to compensate for that past, it is necessary to realize this is impossible. **Only self-forgiveness can heal the past.** If you have been a poor father and husband, in your first marriage, it does not vindicate you to your first wife and the children of that marriage, to be a good father to another wife and children. Only self-forgiveness can free a father from past failures, along with a determination to change and be a better person.

THE SHADOW SIDE OF THE HEALER

Healers need to recognize, own and forgive their dark shadow side, so they do not project it upon those they seek to heal. To have a balanced view of illness, a healer can recognize an illness is not the enemy. Illness may be just what an individual needs to experience, to come to a shift in consciousness that would not have happened without it. **There are clear ways to decipher what the meaning is beneath an illness, but there is always a mystery involved as well. It is essential to avoid blaming or judging anyone for the presence of an illness, and to discourage any such judgment by the ill individual. It does no one any good to blame themselves for an illness or to blame others who may have caused the pain beneath it.**

To heal ourselves and others we can notice those incidents of negative ego pattern which contain various versions of the original one. It does not matter whether we are healing the original negative pattern or some later version of it. Since the healing of any version of a negative pattern has a holographic healing affect upon both body and mind. The healing of childhood shame for instance, can prevent a woman from projecting upon her husband the circumstances and anger she never resolved in her childhood from an abusive father. This woman will no longer allow such abuse and its stressful experiences, as she no longer believes she deserves to be treated in an abusive way.

Becoming a healer is part of my light shadow and has helped me grow into a more compassionate, forgiving, courageous and kind person. I have learned to be effective as a healer, it is necessary to be sensitive to the consensus beliefs concerning an illness an individual has accepted without conceding to them. One such belief is the common one that says illness is merely physical, and the sick individual is a powerless victim.

To be an effective healer, it is necessary to maintain an attitude **of compassionate detachment** in which we respect our boundaries and those of the people we seek to help. If our boundaries are too open, we will experience burnout from not taking care of ourselves. Part of this detachment is refusing to be responsible for the outcome of the choices a sick individual makes. It is disrespectful to approach an ill people with a pitying attitude for this does not empower them to face difficult circumstances.

Burn-out in our work as a healer is a common issue that needs to be addressed by taking the necessary time and space to come to a better balance. Some of the signs of burn-out are exhaustion, uncharacteristic irritability, lethargy, impatience, excessive need for sleep, and unexplained feelings of depression. When burn-out occurs it is often related to an unrealistic belief you are indispensable to your clients. This belief needs to be owned, forgiven and changed to a more humble, healthier one.

THE DARK SHADOW OF ADDICTIONS

Addictions are the allies of our negative egos and the enemy of our shadows. The shadow self encourages us to stop hiding behind our addictions, so we can become genuine and true to ourselves. Addictions such as those for drugs or food are a temporary way of surviving and give us a feeling of freedom temporarily from whatever it is we think we cannot face. We give our power away to whatever substance outside ourselves we depend upon to survive.

Sonya, an elementary teacher, was addicted to both marijuana and food. She used both to help her deal with a deep sense of hollowness and despair. Her belief was," I can never become the artistic person I am capable of being." The drugs instead of inspiring her to paint caused her to be lethargic and hungry. The drugs also helped her tolerate visits to her cranky old mother who depended upon her for morale support. Sonya was so tired after her work day she seldom had enough energy to focus upon the art she loved.

To begin to heal, Sonya recognized how she robbed herself of her talent and power as an artist, by her large consumption of food and drugs. The drugs and food she consumed were expensive, unhealthy and prevented her from living in a safe neighborhood. As a consequence, Sonya had insomnia at night because of anxiety concerning her safety. She seldom went outside to walk, be in nature, or enjoy the sunshine because of her fear of the neighborhood in which she lived. As a result of her addictions and sedentary life-style, she was overweight and weak. She had little energy to focus upon the art projects she wished to do.

Sonya faced both her addictive pattern with its negative beliefs, "I am weak," "I don't know how to love enough," and "I don't deserve to be happy and free." She recognized these beliefs were her mother's, and in many ways she disapproved them. Sonya was a successful teacher; she had many loving friends who intimately cared about her welfare. It was her negative ego she needed to confront and from whom she needed to confront and take back her energy. This negative ego told her, "Go ahead smoke more, you need it."

To heal an addiction, addicted individuals needs to have compassion for themselves and then realize in forgiving themselves, once this addictive substance gave them freedom and was a way of coping with their pain. Now this addictive substance has become their prison. An addicted individual needs to ask: **What is it I am hiding from and afraid to face?** Is it a pain from my childhood about belonging or esteeming myself? Is it some painful memory of abuse that now I am strong enough to face?

An essential step in recovery is to **take an inventory of the costs of your addiction**. What do you have to give up to keep this addiction? Are the costs worth holding on to it?

Then ask for help-not pity-Realize that there are other people who have faced their addictions and can help you. Ask for help from family and friends, your spiritual forces, and from those who have conquered their addictions.

SHADOW WORK-CHAPTER FIVE

1. How did your reaction to your traumatic experiences change your beliefs about life and yourself? What is a more positive truer belief about life and yourself?

2. Recognize, own and forgive yourself, for the negative beliefs or hidden agendas you have to make sense of your traumatic experiences.

3. What is the true, healthier agenda that can replace this hidden agenda? How does this true agenda help you become healthier?

4. If you are addicted to some substance, ask yourself what you love the most? What part of you is lost, broken or rejected? Love and forgive this part.

5. Recognize under depression (anger you believe will get you in trouble) is a higher risk of heart disease. Express your anger honestly and appropriately.

6. Where are you now on the tiers of emotion? Recognize, feel and lift off to at least one or two places beyond by focusing upon this emotion for at least twenty minutes to feel and release it and move to a higher level.

Chapter Six

The Healthy, Light Shadow

*T*he truly frightening aspects of the shadow are not its darkness but its light. This light shadow brings with it a vulnerability, responsibility, and strength that such an admission requires. When we seek to be more powerful, it is the shadow both light and dark we can turn to as it is the best, most elegant source of our power. To experience and empower ourselves with our light shadow, we must first go through our dark shadow, and lift to a higher tier of emotion to allow more expansive feelings of hope, trust, happiness, enthusiasm, optimism and love that wait for us above our pains and constrictions.

THE HEALTHIER BALANCE OF
THE LIGHT SHADOW

Carl Jung called the encounter with the shadow, "the apprentice piece" in an individual's development. This piece then needed to be followed by working with the "anima" which Jung called the "masterpiece." We can view the "anima" or the woman within both men and women as also part of our shadow selves; it is most closely related to the soul which is feminine that is denied in our modern culture. The light shadow holds: all the power you pretend you don't have, your motivation that is fuelled by your love, desire and intimacy, the strength that embarrasses you, and your reliability, true security, spiritual character, and real work based upon your love, caring and intimacy.

Our light shadows also contain all the feminine energy in both men and women such as imagination, creativity, wonder, feeling and conception we have denied because we identified as inappropriate to our sex or because a woman felt these qualities within her were devalued or rejected by her family or culture. Similarly, our light shadows contain all the masculine energies of dynamic action, understanding, will and determination. If you are female and raised in a family that values feminine values over masculine ones, you might reject the cultural values usually associated with males or the masculine sex. Feminine and masculine energy are interrelated not only in our bodies but in our psyches.

When yin energies suffer within any individual, yang energies are also crippled and cannot find a true expression. Thus masculine energies are manifested as frustration, struggle and pain, instead of effective, productive actions. When the feminine energy of dreams, passions, desires, intuitions and visions are suppressed, the power and motivation of masculine energy is emasculated. What values are emphasized are reason, logic, and an impossible perfectionism, competition, comparison, duty and obligations. Without the inspiration of feminine energy, the power of masculine energy is impotent, a facsimile of its real, dynamic power.

When we lose the power of the feminine energies of imagination, desire and vision, we lose our passions, inspirations, compassion, and spiritual values. When duties and obligations are not chosen or preferred then they become unending, we are never able to escape them or find our true selves. What is missing in the shadow of our culture is the juice or life that fuels and come from a fully used imagination. The things that are denied, devalued or suppressed are imagination itself which is called "just fantasy" or only imaging. This paradigm also denies the body and the elegance that comes with receiving help, grace and spiritual worth from a friendly universe.

Balanced people reject traditional ways of feeling and thinking that are chauvinistic, negative or limiting to their uniqueness. They reject the pressures of the competitive, aggressiveness common in western society that is stressful to them. They create other productive ways of life to replace them. A life without pain and struggle goes against the puritan ethic most of us have been taught from our parents and our culture that says "there is no gain without pain or struggle."

A balanced person is at peace within and leading a happy, successful life. Both balanced women and men share certain important feminine and masculine characteristics. They are detached from their negative feelings because they live in an intense way and are grounded in their present reality. They express their feelings appropriately and honestly, with a tact and discrimination that does not harm others or themselves. Through their activity and dreams, they discover the meaning in life. Balanced people are in the process of reaching the deepest levels of feminine (not female) perception where they have a vision of what life can be and their oneness with it.

Healing requires honestly facing and accepting where ever we are upon our life paths, and however dark these paths are for us in the present, there is a reason and purpose for hope beyond. The light shadow requires that we accept the responsibility, vulnerability and strength that the admission of our good, healthy talents and abilities imply. The light shadow holds things such as the power we pretend we don't have, the motivation we have to love, the strength we have to get things done, our reliability and trustworthiness, our loyalty to friends and family, our spiritual character and faithfulness, out real work based upon our natural talents and abilities.

It is my belief that children are not born with blank slates; every infant is born with an intact blueprint for their physical and mental life. The destiny of each individual encompasses where he or she wants to go in this life time and why each one wishes to go there. Our fate is our fundamental choices and beliefs. Our fortune is our relationship to abundance. Our identity is how we define ourselves. The unknown mystery within our shadow is consciously chosen by us before our birth to help us grow. Each one of us has a destiny or blueprint for our lives that is dynamic and ever-changing. The shadow carries this mystery including our past choices, motivation and momentum.

When people lose touch with their souls and the power of choice they lose touch with their destiny. Then their destinies can be attached to pain and sorrow. When we are aware of our destiny, this awareness motivates us with a thrill of enthusiasm. If we are confused as to what our destiny is, one way to discover it is to pursue those activities in which we feel passion, and which give us keen enjoyment. The seeking our true purpose helps us replace frustration and anger with a feeling of well being. A major illness can be the dark night of the soul that can help us realize and own the blockages between who we are and what we can be. One of my purposes in life is that of a healer. In this capacity, I am aware that my methods of healing are considered alternative. It is my conviction that medicine in the future will focus on whatever anyone does mentally, emotionally, and spiritually to heal, rather than upon just temporarily removing symptoms.

INTEGRITY IN HEALING DARK AND LIGHT SHADOW ISSUES

One of the attributes of being a person of integrity is you make a space in your consciousness where you recognize your dark and light shadows, so you can own and be responsible

for it, then forgive yourselves, and choose to heal your dark shadow and to use your light shadow. Integrity is also an essential component of self-esteem; it is learning to motivate your self out of your own desires and expectations rather than from those of others. Integrity helps you be true to your own life path and to your unique abilities.

Margaret knew she had the automatic, conditioned response to try to control other people and herself. She was afraid of making a mistake so tried to control to prevent this from happening. Meanwhile, she ruined her relationships by trying to control others. Her creativity was also constricted by her controlling attitude. To heal herself, whenever she began to feel anxious and had the urge to control, she recognized she had a choice she could try to control or make another choice. Margaret learned to trust herself and remember when she tried to control others she was not being the loving person she truly was.

Margaret recognized whenever she got afraid that she was unable to help her friends or family when they needed help, she would get angry and start trying to control them by telling them what she wanted them to do or be. Instead of helping them, they reacted by getting angry at her controlling behavior. By recognizing this automatic, learned behaviour was controlling and harmful, Margaret recognized, owned, and stopped doing this behavior. She instead listened to what her family and friends needed and was more empathetic and truly helpful.

Margaret faced her fear of making mistakes by telling herself what mattered when she made a mistake, was to take responsibility for that mistake, feel remorse for it, and be responsible for its consequences. Margaret suffered from exhaustion and had the inner image of herself as a warrior like Joan of Arc who had difficulty trusting others or her own inner guidance. To heal herself from exhaustion, Margaret began to trust her inner guidance more and to have more integrity and self-esteem.

She dialogued with the part of herself that insisted on struggling-the warrior part of herself telling it why she no longer needed it to feel safe. Margaret was a spiritual seeker who through meditation got in touch with the part of herself that was connected and quiet. When she had the urge to struggle she called upon this quiet side of herself to direct and help her find the best, most elegant solution to her problems.

Humans live in a universe of free will, choice and duality. We differ from the animals in our ability to look at ourselves and our behavior and to be able to change and to consciously heal ourselves. Animals lack this ability to reflect and to choose to change. Human beings have both a self and an ego. The function of an ego is to bring us information from the outside world that our self then chooses to interpret. When we allow our egos to interpret this information, by refusing to interpret it, our egos become negative. Animals depend upon their instincts to determine their behavior. Our egos are important even though arrested or shamed because they replace our instincts and allow us to reflect upon our lives and behaviours. Humans have the ability to recognize the negative ego patterns that are sources of inner stress. Just as we can change unhealthy patterns of eating, drinking or smoking we can also change negative ego patterns.

Accepting Physical Disabilities as Challenges to Grow

There is a reason for physical disabilities that has to do with our soul's plan for our growth. We may have chosen before our births to focus on certain areas rather than others, and to do this we chose a body or mind that does not function normally. That reason lies in the abilities we are free and open for us to pursue.

An illness may be part of our life plan as it gives us challenges to grow that we might not have otherwise had.

I once supervised a blind therapist, named Colleen, who had a spiritual depth and an ability to access guidance easily through her inner feminine and masculine guides. These guides have helped her get through many times of despair and depression. At one point in our work together, I asked her, if she thought she might have chosen to be born blind to get in touch with her inner world in a way few other people have. Colleen without hesitation answered that she had no doubt this was true.

Without the support of her inner guidance, she did not think she would have been able to cope with her blindness, or would she have achieved as much as she had. In her past times of depression and despair, her inner guides were loyal and ever present friends to her. Her blindness also helped her focus upon her talent as a singer, composer and performer of music; Colleen feels that her music has given her another medium besides counselling through which she can inspire and heal others.

Colleen accepted her blindness, not as a punishment or a misfortune, but as an avenue to accomplish a deep spiritual connection. Her blindness has also helped other blind and sighted people she counsels. Her blindness was part of the light shadow of her body. I have observed that children have a personality when they are born that is present in potential from their birth. Their environment also brings out what is already there.

Whatever our life situations are we have chosen it for a reason. If it involves circumstances that cannot be changed physically then we have chosen to enhance and use other abilities in more intense, concentrated way. The main point of these so called "disabilities" or liabilities is not to focus upon them but to concentrate instead upon the abilities we do have.

Loving and Transforming the
Lesser Parts of Ourselves

It is easy to love the beautiful parts of us, but it is a challenge to love the ugly parts, one of which is our illnesses. We can accept an illness as a lesser part of our identity and to learn from it valuable lessons. By loving these lesser, ugly parts of us, we bring them out of hiding and can deal with them, so they stop blocking our growth and good health. We can listen to the voice of a bodily symptom and it will often tell us what it represents in our life and whether or not it will consent to disappear if we give it what it needs.

One of the reasons we have difficulty transforming the lesser parts of ourselves is that we fear our inner selves, both our subconscious and unconscious minds. We often make the mistake of thinking of our inner world as our dark shadow, the part of us we are afraid to admit or confront. An essential step in healing and transforming the lesser parts of ourselves that are dark because they block our growth and well being is to contact them in meditation and feel and express compassion and love for them.

To love the child, adolescent, ego and objector-protector parts of us, we can recognize these parts of us helped us survive difficult times. We can love the imagination and creativity of our inner child and the fierce determination of our adolescent selves. Even though these lesser parts of us have been responsible for messing up our lives and fostering an unhealthy environment, they did help us survive and live through abuse, abandonment and neglect. The ego may be arrested and shamed, but it is what replaces animal instincts by bringing us messages from our environment. We can love our lesser selves who helped us survive, but at the same time we reject their beliefs and feelings.

In meditation or through journaling, we can dialogue with our inner child, adolescent, negative ego or objector-protector to transform them. The objector-protector, superego part of us, may object to taking the risk to love someone for fear we might get hurt. We can thank the objector-protector for its protection in the past, but tell it this objection is no longer needed. We are strong enough to know when it is safe to love someone, so love is possible again. We may need to go where our inner child or adolescent hides to assure them it is safe to be more imaginative and less filled with suffering, struggling and stress. By bringing our lesser selves out of hiding, they bring some of our shadow issues into the light where we can deal with them in a positive way.

We can forgive these parts of us and have compassion for them when we remember they helped us survive the difficult times of our childhood and adolescence.

To heal our weak, negative ego, we can separate it from us through imagery. We can learn to recognize and own this part of us, and then refuse to give it power, or believe its messages. This may be the part of us that is phoney, untrustworthy, manipulative and ugly to see. When we shove down this dark, ugly part of ourselves, and deny and ignore it, it must come at us through people and events which eventually make us feel undeserving. We then live our lives in a stressful, struggling way. We live as though we don't deserve.

THE CREATIVE-MAGICAL LIFE-STYLE THAT DIMINISHES STRESS

Living an elegant lifestyle is not a new concept; it is an ancient concept that knows that good health and happiness flow from spontaneity rather than the rigidity of stress. The Tao way of life is an ancient tradition based upon a balance of yin and yang energies that results in a wholeness of self or the discovery of the God self within. A life without struggle (not effort) is more balanced, because it expects and gets help from a friendly universe. The balanced person believes he or she can create a friendly world and therefore need not control the people in their world.

The Tao Te Ching is an ancient Taoist text which compares the Tao or movement of God to water who gives life to a thousand things but does not strive. The Tao is like water; it is the source of all things, yet it is without form.

This Taoist text defines the healthiest, most harmonious life as one with out stress and struggle. It is my belief and experience that contrary to consensus beliefs there is an alternative life-style which is less stressful and full of struggles and more natural and gracious. This life-style is healthier because it is based upon spontaneity and self-trust rather than stress and struggle. This spontaneity has its own order when we follow the path of our own unique, creative impulses. These impulses though unique to each of us are also what will help us contribute most to the larger society.

Not only is this life-style the most harmonious, creative and healthy; it is also a magical one. We all do create our lives using our imagination, will, expectation and desire, but some people do so consciously. Many people create their lives unconsciously. When people create unconsciously they often deny and hide the ugliness and negativity in the dark shadow of their bodies. The body holds this shadow for them; in time if this shadow is not expressed and resolved, it may be expressed in the form of tumors, disease, and malfunctioning organs.

Einstein once said that the most important question you could ever ask is "Is it a friendly universe?" If you believe the universe is a friendly to you, it will be. Einstein was a patent office bureaucrat who believed in a friendly universe. His theories concerning the relationship of matter to energy were accepted by other physicists, even though he had no academic credentials or mathematical proofs. Each of us has our own talents and personal genius that can be discovered and used.

The choice to be healthier and live longer may depend upon deciding to live a less stressful life-style. This means instead of repressing creative impulses, each of us begins to trust these impulses are good and wise. Then we can experience the joy that comes when synchronicities and miracles large and small happen. This attitude trusts, as Einstein did, the universe as basically friendly. Einstein was a lowly clerk in a patent office whose reputation was based upon some papers he wrote which caused other physicists to accept his genius and recognize him as their equal.

Whether or not we are able to use this creative framework is based upon whether we trust there is a field of well-being in which spiritual forces support us when we ask for help. This means we say "No" to negative ego beliefs that we are alone, separate and without help. This help is available to anyone who is free of destructive religious, cultural or scientific beliefs. This creative framework is the source from which nature springs and allows a freedom in which images, thoughts and healing can manifest with a minimal amount of effort and time. The first step to access this help is to state our desires, purposes and intentions.

This creative framework is not neutral; it is as close to us as our impulses and depends upon a wise faith in its presence and willingness to respond. This life-style depends upon a belief that we as physical, human beings are also spiritual beings whose basic nature is good and creative. Therefore, the impulses that flow from this nature are also good. In this trusting context, we then allow ourselves to respond and act upon our inner creative impulses. These impulses may be to read a particular book, to make a phone call, to befriend a certain person, or attend a certain meeting.

When we do listen and act upon our creative impulses, synchronicities and coincidences occur that bring magical events into our lives. We then experience more success with less struggle and stress. We then live with elegance; **elegance means that you spend the least amount of energy both physically and spiritually for the maximum amount of return to realize your purposes and goals in life**. Twenty minutes of focused programming and processing can set in motion the healing of a disease or the manifestation of a creative project.

Relaxation rather than stress activates the creative process within this life-style. This means we have faith that when we ask for help to heal or manifest something, help will come. The end result may take an entirely different form than we expected. The consensus reality ethic is one that sees stress and a pit-bull approach to life as the only way to reach goals and become successful. My family were immigrants from Sweden and they lived and taught me to believe in the necessity of a struggling life-style, both by their example and beliefs.

My parents believed there was nobility in struggle; they taught me to accept that struggle was necessary to achieve and survive. As a result of this stressful, life-style of hard work and struggle my father, Torsten Holmstrom, died in his mid-forties from heart disease. My mother Martha also suffered from varicose veins in her legs and a neurological disease that caused her to have head tremors in her later years. Both worked harder than they should have and suffered the consequences.

Most of my life I have struggled in various ways to learn a profession, to heal myself and others. It has been only in the last ten or twenty years that I have learned a new way to deal with the challenges that life has brought me in my efforts to become what I was meant to be. I have learned that the friendly universe does help bring me what I ask for in a way that is much less stressful than my previous, pit-bull, nose-to-the- grindstone life-style. To let go of the struggle and stress of the past, I have learned to accept the chaos and confusion that is necessary in any creative healing project. My dark shadow self knew very well how to do silent suffering and struggle. My new life-style is based upon trust that this universe is friendly to me.

LEARNING TO ALLOW AND RECEIVE INSTEAD OF STRESS AND STRUGGLE

In the Cartesian beliefs of our consensus reality, we are each an observer, separate from the reality of our world and bodies. These beliefs deny the findings of modern quantum physics which tell us each of us is an active participant in creating our health and world. We all have resisted the possibility of receiving and allowing because our cultural paradigms insist that receiving does not fit into a system of cause and effect and its emphasis on competition, comparison and the nobility of struggle. To allow and receive, rather than stress and struggle, we need to be aware that receiving is not the opposite of doing. Neither is it a passive process. Receiving is actually more active than doing, but is a higher octave of doing. Receiving is neither doing nor being; it is somewhere between these two.

To lift to a higher less stressful continuum of living, we can face the underlying cultural, chauvinistic views that reject receiving and allowing as too feminine, not logical and rational enough, with their insistence on singular masculine authority. This cultural stance limits imagination, and with it the power of will. Some of the other resistances to receiving are our negative ego imprints of control, needing approval, or revenge. If we refuse to trust or use our imagination we will not be open and available to receive help or healing.

When we lack forgiveness of ourselves for creating the environment that allows an illness, we resist its healing. One of my friends, Lori has learned to allow and receive healing through forgiveness. Lori is a psychologist who has helped many. When her marriage ended and she became ill, Lori was at the lowest point of her life. In the summer of 2003, she was in a nursing home and in great pain while recovering from two surgeries. She was neglected, ill, and dying and asking for help when Jenny, a practical nurse, one of her former clients, suddenly appeared to bath, nurture and heal her.

Lori felt deeply graced and now uses what she learned about forgiveness in this health crisis to help others. These include orphans in Rwanda who have experienced the cruelty of genocide in which their parents were killed and they were raped, mutilated or terrorized by their neighbors. One of the essential steps of forgiveness is to stop feeling separate and to feel we are loved and loving.

Living a struggling life is a by product of feeling undeserving. To heal this pattern of struggle and stress, it is necessary to understand that undeserving comes in waves with ebbs and flows. The key to healing undeserving is to realize that it is not determined by merit but by willingness to receive. One of the hiding places for an unconscious wave of undeservability is our dark and light shadow. When we refuse to look at the dark ugly sides of ourselves because we are afraid this is too dangerous, then this side of us is wrapped up and contained in undeserving. This attitude says, "I refuse to see my ugliness, so I assume I don't deserve." This unconscious wave also can hide a light shadow in which we deny the beautiful, powerful, loving side of ourselves. One way to heal this undeserving is to work with the part of us who remembers we are loved.

TRUSTING SPONTANEITY

The functioning of our bodies occurs with an unconscious spontaneity, yet an underlying order. We each think and speak without knowing how. We digest and circulate blood without a rational thought. When unimpeded with repressions of thought and feeling, our bodies function well.

Spontaneity is impossible if we are trying to control ourselves through struggle and rigid control. When we feel so frightened we act compulsively, or repress our physical motion, or our self expression.

The dark, shadow side of many cultural and religions beliefs have fostered the fear of the spontaneous, inner self and its creative manifestations. These troublesome religious beliefs foster the concept of the sinful self who is contaminated and thus driven by evil. These beliefs make it impossible for people to trust the spontaneity of their inner selves. These concepts have also been accepted by psychological theories such as Freudian psychology which assumes our inner selves, both our subconscious and unconscious are filled with unsavory sexual impulses and desires.

Under the shadow of negative beliefs concerning the unsavory nature of our inner selves, the idea of trusting the inner self as innocent, good and healthy seems to be unwise. However, the spontaneous, creative person soon finds that real discipline is the result of true spontaneity. Much more quality work is achieved by creative people when they relax and consult their inner guidance about what next to do or explore.

The imbalance that occurs as a consequence of harsh discipline leads to an unnecessary stress on the body. Any extreme of behavior such as overeating, over drinking, or excessive exercising is punishing to the body. Errors of thought and belief are often at the source of a health problem especially the belief that we need to punish ourselves to be healthy or spiritual. Often those errors are related to a fear of using a particular power or of spontaneity itself because of the fear that inner impulses are evil.

When we trust ourselves to become more spontaneous in our thoughts and actions, then more synchronistic events begin to occur that can give us the experience of the Tao acting within our lives. "Synchronicity" is a descriptive term for the link between two events that are connected through their meaning; this link cannot be explained by cause and effect. Jung described an incident with one of his patients who always took an over rational approach to her life that prevented her from a deeper human understanding. This woman had just told him of a dream she had in which a scarab, or beetle had appeared. Just then there was a wrap upon the window and Jung opened the window to present her with her scarab.

Synchronicity involves meaningful events in which a person gives meaning to a coincidence in which an actual event coincided with a thought, vision, dream or premonition. Meaningful coincidence such as the one described touch a deep feeling level in the psyche that many modern authors equate with the Tao of ancient wisdom. When we learn to trust our inner self, we have more of these synchronicities that help us know we are connected and our lives are being guided from unseen forces.

To be optimally healthy does not mean only the absence of illness. It means we are creative in seeking and realizing our life purposes. True creative discipline grows out of spontaneity, trust and seeking. It is erroneous to think of creative spontaneity as opposite to discipline; there is a creative discipline propelled by passion. Creative people will tell you their inspirational ideas were often conceived one morning when they were walking, or sitting relaxing, or while they were taking a shower and preparing for the day.

Creativity gives us a greater vitality because it is fuel for our bodies and souls. The source of creativity is feminine energy. Our souls are a feminine energy that uses the language of imagination, passion, symbols and images. A denial of feminine energy such as imagination, intuition or emotion, blocks its messages in both men and women. When we do not listen to our dreams, intuition, or experiences, our shadow-souls may speak to us in illness. The solutions to problems and creative ideas often bubble up from the unconscious in mysterious ways beyond our conscious control. A solution or idea can also come from a book we just happen to find, or from a person who just happens to appear in our life to tell us something important.

Harnessing Our Unconscious and Subconscious Minds for Healing

We are not controlled by unconscious conditioning unless we believe we are. A mature mind accepts information from both the inner mind and exterior world. We are not cut off from our unconscious minds unless we believe we are. Interactive guided imagery and music is a healing technique I use to induce a relaxed state to communicate with the subconscious and unconscious for healing purposes. It differs from hypnotherapy by encouraging patients to follow their own imaginations to heal an illness.

We do not need to fear our inner minds are evil or dark; we are not at the mercy of our inner minds. Turning inward can be initially done with the help of a therapist such as myself, because I help the client both relax, then focus upon getting information and giving direction to the health problem to find a resolution. The light and dark shadows, being all we deny or do not like about ourselves, are found most often within our unconscious minds, so it is necessary to understand how we can access and harness the power within our unconscious to consciously heal ourselves.

It is also the unconscious mind that is closest to those emotions both dark and light that affect our bodies and health. To understand the power of the unconscious mind, it is necessary to know that its power transcends time and space and the limitations of reason and logic. Therefore, it can never be completely understood by the conscious or rational mind. Nevertheless, we can access the power of the unconscious in a number of ways, particularly through harnessing it through choice.

Dr. Andrew Weil has great enthusiasm for interactive guided imagery as a healing method because he has observed how effective it is to heal illness for his patients and members of his family. He tells the story of how his wife Sabine when she was seven months pregnant with his first child (her fourth) was having back problems and feared a difficult childbirth. A friend used guided imagery to help Sabine speak to her unborn child and to her painful back. As a result of this interaction, her back problem disappeared and her childbirth experience was less difficult. Sabine became aware that her back was angry and wanted her to place warm packs upon it rather than cold ones. She asked her back whether it would be willing to stop hurting if she did this. Her back agreed and from this point on in her pregnancy she no longer experienced back pain.

Dr. Weil states in his book *Spontaneous Healing* that no disease process is beyond the reach of therapies that use interactive guided imagery work. He recommends working with a trained professional to ensure this method is used correctly. It is Dr. Weil's opinion that guided imagery work can enhance the effectiveness of other treatments including the use of allopathic drugs and surgery, but he states he finds it particularly effective for all autoimmune disorders and for any illness in which healing seems to blocked or stalled.

I agree with Dr. Weil that the imagery chosen to treat a disease needs to be that which has an emotional impact. The use of special music with a positive resonance to a person also helps the ill person be more emotionally involved in the guided imagery experience. Before working with a client I explore what images and music are particularly emotionally moving to that person.

Everyone who is conscious has an unconscious mind. We all have a conscious, subconscious and unconscious mind. Of these three, the unconscious mind is the most powerful and the most conscious. The unconscious mind holds the record of our past lives and sometimes the reason we have certain disabilities or illnesses. I have had success in helping heal a respiratory illness of a young woman who felt it was related to experiences in the gas chambers of Germany. As a result of finding the young man she was in that previous lifetime and helping him forgive himself, she healed the respiratory problem she had in this life time.

There is an intricate balance of power between the conscious mind and the subconscious and unconscious. The conscious mind is the only one that is capable of choice, and therefore it has the power to direct the more powerful subconscious and unconscious minds. The conscious mind although the least powerful and conscious is the captain, the one who steers the giant ship of our consciousness. Our core beliefs, often those we decided to hold during childhood are stored for us in the subconscious. These core beliefs were made to help us survive difficult childhood experiences. As we mature, we can consciously discover and change these beliefs if they are detrimental to our health, happiness or well being.

Our bodies are our temples and the product of our creativity. We each create our bodies on a daily basis by what we choose to focus upon. The condition of our health is an extension of our creativity and speaks loudly of what we believe to be true. We may desire good health, but believe in our poor health. Through our conscious beliefs and thoughts we focus like the lens of a camera to direct the flow of our unconscious processes which then bring these beliefs and thoughts into reality.

If we are focused upon thoughts and beliefs upon illness, we will be ill. To heal, we need to be convinced of our ability to change our beliefs and thoughts to healthier ones. Quite fundamentally, to be healthy, we have to believe in health. Our conscious beliefs affect our bodies continually. Many of our beliefs are blue prints with mental pictures that our bodies respond to both on conscious and unconscious levels. Illness may be an experience that serves our purposes in ways we may not wish to admit. Some of the pay-offs of illness are issues of control, self-protection, self-pity or self-punishment.

The power of the unconscious is immense as it is the most conscious part of us. Many have denied the existence of the unconscious or dismissed its power by saying it could not be utilized because it was unconscious. We cannot harness all of the enormous powers of our unconscious minds, but we can harness enough of it to influence the resonance or frequency of energy around ourselves that then creates our bodies. We can consciously choose to let go of toxic beliefs and emotional patterns. Through focusing upon the powerful energies of love, power, imagination and creativity, we are more healthy and happy.

Carl Jung was a psychiatrist who knew and had experienced the power of the unconscious in his own experiences and those of his clients; he knew how the unconscious presence becomes conscious in many symbolic and metaphorical ways, particularly through dream images. Jung was aware of how the unconscious dream images of a dreamer often point to the need to balance some conscious stance. In a dream, a woman who feels impotent, may find herself driving a semi-truck. Her light shadow in the unconscious is thus telling her she is much more powerful than she allows herself to know.

One of the main reasons people do not heal is they do not have an image or an understanding of a healthier pattern of thought and feeling. They have not identified the negative ego pattern that is unhealthy, nor have they imagined or conceived of a healthy one to replace it. This healthier pattern lies within their light shadow that holds for them the potentiality of its realization. This light shadow-part of their soul has picked up those things the individual has discarded over the years that would make this possible.

James, a fifty year old banker, as a child discarded his potential for feelings. His parents taught him that a child was to be as quiet as possible-to be seen and not heard when he was home. As a consequence James learned early to inhibit his feelings. His father was a Norwegian farmer who firmly believed that to be a man it was noble to be as quiet, stoical and as unfeeling as possible.

Unfortunately, this kind of stoical inhibited behavior set James up for the kind of inhibited emotional pattern that stuffs anger. James was not even aware when he was experiencing anger. He had no vocabulary to describe his emotions, particularly his anger and irritation at others. James had been neglected as a child and as a result had a pattern of fear, resentment and anger in place of love. He was uncomfortable and afraid to express his loving feelings to his wife.

In his mid-fifties, James experienced a heart attack that caused him to become more aware of his pattern of suppression of his feelings particularly his anger. To heal himself, James had to give himself permission to express his anger at his life in an honest and appropriate way. He then had to replace this angry mode of existence with more nurturing from his imaginative, tender and creative side. James found he enjoyed creating with the use of clay. He allowed his imagination to express with clay the feelings he had and his need to find beauty. This craft helped him feel and express his emotions more.

BELIEFS THAT PROMOTE GOOD HEALTH

Children naturally approve and love themselves, until taught differently. We all begin life approving of ourselves and our bodies, but we often learn to feel distrust of ourselves and our bodies by the influence of our parents or peers. It is helpful to remember when healing ourselves of any disease or malady, we need to start with the innocent freshness of our childhood to reawaken our earlier attitudes of goodness, trust and hope for the future. Healthy beliefs on the surface may seem naïve or childish. However, these beliefs are based upon a wise innocence that transcends consensus reality.

Healthy beliefs are those that affirm that we are each a valuable part of the universe and that our existence enriches those around us and all creation. Healthy beliefs are based upon the knowledge that it is good, natural, and safe for us to grow, develop and use our abilities. By doing so, we enrich not only our lives but the lives of others and the earth. Beliefs in self-sacrifice are thought to be noble and honorable especially by those who already feel limited by their social status and position. When someone purposely gives up their life for another, they hold the inner destructive belief that their life is not valuable. Healthy beliefs are based upon a trust that each of us is eternally supported by the universe of which we are a part. A formative principle of this trust is by nature we are good and deserving, as are all living things. We are each a beloved child of the universe, both ancient and young at once, with an identity beyond the annuals of time.

SHADOW WORK-CHAPTER SIX-
THE HEALTHY LIGHT SHADOW

1. What do you fear most about your light shadow? What power is hidden in it you refuse to own and take as your responsibility to use and heal?

2. Do you conform to a chauvinistic cultural myth of what you should be? How imaginative, feeling, vulnerable, and self-confident are you in expressing both your masculine and feminine energies?

3. What beliefs do you have that prevent you from being as open and trusting as you were as a child?

4. What light, luminous intent lies beneath your physical symptoms or illnesses? Ask what you get from this illness until you see the light. Take this luminous intent, and ask what it does to the darkness? If it is self-pity you wish, what does the luminous intent of self-reliance do to self-pity?

5. What are the fulcrum issues that most often cause you to be off balance?

6. What handicap or illness do you have that helps you see your light shadow?

7. As an antidote to lack of forgiveness, be grateful for moments of beauty in you daily life. Record these until gratitude comes naturally.

Chapter Seven

Healing of Heart Disease during the Shadow-Middle Years

*T*he shadow reflects back to us through the crises of illness the fact that our life-style and personal patterns need to be changed as they are no longer working and are unhealthy. The leading cause of death from heart attack often occurs in the middle years and can be prevented because these attacks are related to life-style and inner issues of hostility, stress and cynicism. A mid-life crisis is a time of profound transition in which many of us need a new orientation.

Heart disease can be prevented by resolving the inner and outer beliefs and stresses which lead to a hostile, lonely, struggling, driven life. Heart attacks are the leading killer of American men and women. These heart attacks kill five hundred thousand people a year. Of the 1½ million heart attacks suffered by Americans each year, nearly half occur between the ages of 45 and 65. Three fifths of these heart attacks are fatal.

The task of the shadow years, the longest period of our lives, after our adolescent wounding to our mid-life crisis in our mid-forties or fifties, is to separate from our origins-our parental traditional spiritual roots so we can be our own individual selves. The purpose of this task is that we learn to parent ourselves, so we can become our own unique selves. From this, we can find our own self created connection to our spirituality-to God/

Goddess/All There Is. The shadow years offer us the opportunity to experience a spiritual rebirth-to consciously create a personal spirituality unique to us.

In our mid-life crises, our shadow brings us situations including those that involve illness to help us face and transform our negative ego based personas into a more spiritually based unique beings. Each of us has personality drives that during the dark night of our souls take us to places in which the ego agendas that have previously driven us may drive us into our own lost dark woods of heart disease. The dark shadow of our hidden agendas of control, our manipulations, false pride, hostility or greed we refuse to own and process during our mid-life crises begin to unravel and find expression within our bodies.

Dr. Dean Ornish, a pioneer in reversing heart disease through life-style changes, discovered that there is something more fundamental to the development of heart disease than high cholesterol, and blood pressure, overweight and little exercise. When he looked at nine large follow up studies in Finland, Sweden, and California, what he discovered to be the most significant risk factor for premature death from heart disease was the lack of intimate social ties. He found the less developed and intimate the social ties of an individual; the more likely was he or she to develop heart disease.

In his book *Love and Survival,* Dr. Ornish tells the story of his own inner conflicts concerning love and intimacy. When he reached his fortieth birthday, he realized there was a big contrast between what he had achieved in the outer world and how happy and fulfilled he felt within. During this midpoint of his life, he realized that he had been looking in the wrong places for his happiness and peace. His great fame and fortune as a heart specialist who had helped thousands through diet and life-style changes reverse their heart disease had not made him happy. At mid-life, Ornish learned how to be truly intimate with significant others. He learned what truly fulfilled him was to open his heart and be more vulnerable in his relationships with himself and other significant loved ones.

Ornish concluded that the real epidemic in our culture is not only physical heart disease, but also what he called emotional and spiritual heart disease-profound feelings of loneliness, isolation, alienation and depression which he observed were so prevalent in our culture. Those institutions of church and family that used to provide a sense of connection and community have broken down and not yet been replaced.

One of the most graphic examples of the importance of a sense of connectedness and community to heart disease is Roseto, Pennsylvania. Roseto was studied intensively for over fifty years. During this time this town had a strikingly low mortality rate from heart attacks during the first thirty years it was studied when compared to a near by town.

The risk factors for heart disease such as smoking, high-fat diet, and diabetes were at least as prevalent in Roseto as in near by communities.

The key to its low mortality rate, researchers discovered was Roseto's stable structure and sense of community and the intimacy of its members, especially their loving life-style. The Italian people in this community knew they were loved and respected as part of the community. When they were sick or needed help they could count upon their neighbors or family to support them. When this stable community structure disintegrated after fifty years, the mortality rates in Roseto became similar to those of the communities around it.

Ornish learned from his own problems with relationships and with helping people reverse their heart disease how essential it was to learn to **be open-hearted and vulnerable.** When we are vulnerable, anger and shame are expressed cleanly rather than kept hidden or denied. Vulnerability essentially means we disclose parts of ourselves that are hidden in our shadows. In the process of being vulnerable, we feel heard, seen and connected. Ultimately, healing occurs when we see with the wisdom of a double vision that knows we are separate, yet paradoxically connected. A heart disease often symbolizes our inability to express our love or our suppressed hostility.

The languages of the world are filled with expressions about the heart that reflect a universal intuitive knowledge about the heart as the center of higher qualities of being such as love, appreciation, compassion and caring. When we throw ourselves into some activity, without considering our full integrity or best interests, we say we are doing it, "without our hearts being in it." When people are sincere in their words, we say, "they are speaking from their hearts," or when they are wise in their actions we say, "they have followed their hearts." When we fall into despair or sorrow we say, "we are disheartened."

Allopathic medicine has traditionally thought of the heart as merely a physical pump, although an important one, only useful for circulating blood throughout the body. In traditional Chinese medicine, the heart is seen as the bridge and connection between mind and body. This medicine says that the heart contains *Shen*, which is translated as both mind and spirit. Thus the mind or spirit is housed in the heart, and the blood vessels are the communication network that carries the heart's messages throughout the body. In both Chinese and Japanese languages the common view of the heart is that it has an intelligence that operates independent of the brain yet in communications with it.

Many spiritual traditions refer to the heart center as the Tifferet, seat of the soul and the connecting place of balance, harmony and beauty between heaven and earth, the spiritual and the humanness within the body. In Ayurvedic medicine, the heart is the center and meeting place of subtle or etheric energies from the lower three chakra and the upper three chakra or energy chakras of the body.

Modern researchers such as those who work in The Institute of HeartMath have confirmed the fact that the heart has its own communication system that can operate independently from that of the mind. The heart is a sensitive organ that has long been known as the center of loving feelings. The one most serious attribute that places people at risk for heart disease is isolation or choosing to live separately from others or nature. This isolation is often related to a hostile, cynical attitude.

The most important factor is the presence of anger that is related to patterns of isolation and pessimism in the form of Type A behavior, especially the hostility associated with it. There is a strong resistance to the idea that our patterns of hostility and isolation may be at the core of heart disease. Shadow work is inherent in any form of heart healing; it is especially important in healing heart disease because traditional medicine does not cure the underlying emotional, mental causes of heart disease.

People who are able to experience more loving feelings such as caring, appreciation and love do live longer and have less symptoms of heart disease. The recurrent rate of arterial blockage after angioplasty is 25-35 percent, while a bypass operation only bypasses the problem, but does not cure it. Most experts have advised a strict change in life-style with diet changes, exercise and avoiding smoking. In fact, it is clear that for many patients, emotional, psychological and even spiritual factors are at least as important, both in preventing and in healing an already damaged heart.

Our hearts connect us to a Divine resonance. The first cells of a fetus are heart cells. The frequency of heart cells is 5,000 times stronger than those of our brains. When we focus upon thoughts of appreciation, joy, love and gratitude, we trigger the limbic, prefrontal cortex, the part of our brains that is active when we are calm, compassionate and balanced. This part of our brains can transcend the automatic, fearful parts of our brains most active in fearful, fight or flight reactions. The prefrontal cortex of our brains can make the choices necessary to transcend negative ego patterns originating in childhood.

DEPRESSION, STRESS AND HEART DISEASE

In a follow up study of 2,000 men in Germany over 13 years, stress and depression were six times more predictive of those who would develop cancer or coronary heart disease than the physical measures of high cholesterol, smoking or high blood pressure. Stress is an emotional state in which one feels threatened in some way. Most harmful is the stress that is chronic over which one feels he has no way to escape or control. Depression is a form of repressed anger in which you feel you will get in trouble for if you express it; it is also a reaction to a sudden change such as moving to a new place. When someone feels depressed over large or seemly insignificant things, it is wise to recognize the source. You can ask yourself, "Is there anger in my life that I will get in trouble for if I express it?" "Has there been a change in my life I have not adapted to?"

These German men were apparently experiencing both anxiety and depression at the some time. The fear response of chronic stress involves the sympathetic nervous system activated by the hypothalamus, pituitary and adrenal glands that in turn stress important organs such as the heart. The anxiety involved in chronic stress is particularly related to cancer because it results in a low functioning immune system. The focus upon external sources of stress activates the muscular and fight-flight, but deactivates the natural function of surveillance of the body for foreign, malignant cells.

Shamans are aware that there are emotional patterns particularly carried from father to son, or mother to daughter that can trigger illnesses such as cancer or heart trouble. Heart disease and cancer run in families. Apart from inherited DNA or genetics there are also psychological characteristics that predispose one to abusive relationships or health problems. Daughters can relive their mother's lives and illnesses and son's can take on the competitive, hostile or stressful life-styles conducive to heart disease and that led to their father's pattern of early mortality.

ANGER, VULNERABILITY AND HEART DISEASE

The most comprehensive work on personality and cardiovascular diseases is that of Friedman, Rosenman and their colleagues in defining and exploring Type A and Type B personalities. Friedman discovered that patients with coronary problems were chronically tense and literally always on the edge of their seats. This observation came from the upholsterer who noticed that chairs in the heart doctor's waiting room were worn only on the front edges, as if they were sitting in tense expectation. These researchers discovered that the heart disease susceptible Type A personalities was differentiated from their healthier Type B counterparts by excessively competitive drive with a continual sense of time urgency. These individuals also showed an easily aroused hostility.

In contrast to Type A behaviour, Type B personalities were more relaxed, and in the long run just as productive and more creative. While Type A personalities took little or no time out for pleasure and vacations, Type B personalities were able to enjoy the vacations, relationships and ordinary daily pleasures more. It is essential that patients with heart disease check themselves for Typical Type A behavior and not only change these behaviors, but also the belief system and feelings related to it. What is most exciting about Friedman's research was he and his associates later proved that Type A personalities could be changed and this change prevented further heart attacks. Through group and educational programs Friedman proved dramatically that those who changed their Type A personality patterns had no or fewer further heart attacks.

MANAGING AND TRANSCENDING STRESS

High stress occupations are dangerous to health. Two major research studies (Kuper 2002 and a 23 year follow up study by Stephenson) found that a person who has high work stress is twice is likely to die of a heart attack than those without this stress. Stress is a complex response to a perceived threat or challenge that includes physical, behavioral, mental and emotional elements. A stressor is a real or imagined thing that sets off the stress process. Humans are unique in being threatened by things that they anticipate that never happened and may never happen. *We are our own biggest source of stress because of what we tell ourselves about our life situations and our abilities to cope with them.*

Any positive, healing approach to stress needs to begin by recognizing what we are telling ourselves about our ability to cope with our life situations. Instead of focusing upon the threats we believe are in our environment, we can turn inward to listen to our own inner guidance and to admit and realize what strengths we have. Each of us is unique and has qualities and talents we can utilize to transcend our perceived threats. We are all much stronger than we realize and have ways to either change the home or work situations we are in or leave them.

Most Americans have some kind of spirituality or religious faith that in times of illness and stress can be called upon to help them find safety, heal and endure their suffering. By turning inward to listen to our inner guidance, our higher selves, better angels, holy spirit or soul, we can transcend the stress of crises. We can turn inward in meditation, prayer or quiet listening for guidance. If you are an individual who is prone to anxiety, you are probably misperceiving the threats in your environment or your ability to cope with them. You may underestimate the resources and social supports that are available to you, and be making cognitive errors by magnifying, personalizing or catastrophing threats in your environment.

The depressed person who has a perception of real or symbolic loss can take time to feel their despair and then face their resistance to change and to use their imagination to explore new possibilities and options. It is important for a depressed people to recognize what negative thoughts they have about themselves, others and the world, so they can determine whether these are healthy ones. The person who is often hostile and angry can develop skills and mindfulness techniques to manage their anger in healthier ways by stopping, to breathe, forgive themselves, and change their hostile thoughts.

HEARTMATH RESEARCH AND
HEALTHIER BALANCE

If we are ill, we can focus upon the fulcrum issue or issues such as wisdom or the dark or light shadow as an antidote to heal us. **The shadow is one of the fulcrum issues that underlie illness. The dark shadow of fear or chronic anxiety can for instance lead to high blood pressure or immune deficiency illnesses.** The healing of any imbalance is a desired state of composure or an emotional and mental focus tempered by balance. Composure or peacefulness is a state of knowing who you are and who you wish to become; it is a state of being calm, steady and tranquil. This peaceful state is continual, not continuous, and is a state of self possession in which you own and are responsible for yourself.

To fully understand the concept of balance in reference to health, we need to recognize that poor health is not only a physical problem; it is also psychological, emotional and spiritual. Someone may be told, he or she needs to have a better balance in their life to be healthy, but seldom are they taught what this means on other than a physical basis. For nearly two decades, the Institute of HeartMath in Boulder Creek, California has researched how heart intelligence can influence stress to bring about a better balance needed for good health.

What Doc Childre and his associates discovered was that the heart is the primary generator of rhythm and balance in the body. The HeartMath Institute has developed tools that have been scientifically tested and proven to bring balance between the mind and emotions, the sympathetic and parasympathetic nervous systems, and the heart and mind. These tools have been proven to lower stress, self-regulate heart beat and blood pressure, and promote more creativity and performance.

The balanced point or fulcrum of our minds is the pause to pay attention, observe, and become more wise and creative. This pause allows us to relax, be in the present, in our bodies and become more aware of our feelings, beliefs, and images.

A fulcrum is a fixed support upon which a level can come to balance. A fulcrum is the pivotal point or issue causing a process to be in or out of balance. There often are more than one issue involved in an imbalance.

The easy-to- use tool called Quick Coherence or Heath Lock consists of only three steps: (1) Heart focus (2) Heart Breathing and (3) Heart Feeling of care, love and appreciation to balance your thoughts and emotions quickly, lower stress and boost your energy, focus and higher mental abilities. This technique and several others such as Freeze Frame and Cut Through are designed to empower and find solutions to problems that call upon a higher level of wisdom than mental processing alone. These techniques have been used in schools, social service agencies and Industry to lower stress, promote emotional and physical balance, and improve health. Twenty-eight percent of the employees of Motorola Company had high blood pressure. After using these techniques regularly their blood pressure and stress hormones returned to normal levels.

The composure and calmness of balance does not mean you are not afraid, but that you have moved beyond the seduction or oppression of the blockages of fear, anger, hurt or self pity. We can acknowledge, own, and forgive ourselves for these blockages and choose instead to be courageous and act and respond, despite not knowing all the answers. A pause to reflect becomes a balance or fulcrum point in which we can notice when our negative ego agendas are present. Then we can decide to reject these responses, forgive ourselves and choose to focus upon other more healthy responses. We then change our emotional environment. This pause to reflect changes the resonance of our emotions. Other fulcrum issues besides that of the shadow are wisdom, guidance, responsibility, direction, love, will and authority. These focus points help us become more balanced. Pausing to reflect is a step in the healing process of any illness.

HEALING HIGH BLOOD PRESSURE AND EXHAUSTION IN MID-LIFE

Donna was a middle-aged woman whose main drive was to be an achiever. Unfortunately this drive had become a compulsion for her. Donna had become so absorbed in achieving as a lawyer that she was exhausted. She felt as though she was sitting in the back seat of her car and her drive to achieve was driving her life. He fellow lawyers took advantage of her abilities because she was so competent that she could do twice or three times the amount of work they could. She had paid a price for this driven condition in having dangerously high blood pressure, chronic migraine headaches and exhaustion.

During her health burn-out, Donna realized she had become a compulsive, workaholic; she felt as though her personal life was unfulfilled, so she made some changes in her work schedule to allow herself to rest, regain her vitality and find herself. She felt lost in a dark wood with the need to find who and what she truly wished to be and do. She realized in her push to achieve she had not allowed herself to nurture herself. As a child, Donna had focused upon earning the love of her mother by trying to achieve something that would get her approval.

Donna as an achiever believed she had to earn her worth and love through successes and achievements. With this attitude is a belief that she was only as worthy as her last achievement. Without the continuous achievement, she believed she had little or no worth. Achievers have issues related to shame at not being good enough. To heal this deep feeling of shame at the base of her shadow self, I asked Donna to write a shame contract with her mother and then to destroy it.

MID-LIFE HEALING CRISES

Donna discovered in writing this contract, that her mother had taught her to be ashamed of her femininity and female body. One of the clauses of this contract was that she like her mother would die of a stroke from a driven overworked life. Donna asked her subconscious for a healing image to help her play and enjoy her life in a more balanced way. The healing image she received was that of a hummingbird. Donna surrounded herself with this image, and through it gradually found more joy, relaxation and health.

As an achiever Donna had problems with being fully in her heart and feelings, therefore she had problems feeling her worthiness and value. She depended upon others for approval especially the senior members of her law firm who praised her for her productivity and commitment to their law firm. As a consequence, Donna had lost her connection with her sense of inner intuition and spiritual guidance. Her heart energy was blocked from receiving nurturing. In its place, she had built a persona identity that gave her a sense of value through the approval of others.

The pain from her migraines and chronic fatigue caused her to pause to feel the despair and emptiness of depending upon the praise of others for her value. The negative ego agenda of her drive had reached its ultimate shadow conclusion. The dark night of her soul in which she felt lost came when she encountered the empty, blank feeling beneath her false beliefs.

Donna opened to the shame and hurt underneath this despair. By facing the shame of depending on the approval of others for her value, she was able to drop the mask of a lonely, super woman. Beyond this loneliness was an authenticity and integrity that came from opening her heart to who she truly was. Donna was able to relax more and feel more acceptance and value within her self. As a consequence, her migraines disappeared and her blood pressure dropped to a normal level.

Before mid-life, the focus of most lives is biological and social in creating a career, a family, home and nurturing children. The second half of life has a different spiritual and cultural focus. This focus is to follow one's own inner guidance to become your unique self. Of particular importance is to place more importance on your personal spiritual relationship rather than a purely religious one, making the changes necessary to be connected to your spirit and soul in whatever form that is most natural to you. To do this it is necessary to let go of negative ego attitudes and beliefs based upon fear, scarcity or cynical beliefs.

When mid-life comes somewhere between the ages of 35 to fifty, it is a time to take an inventory of what matters most to us by asking questions of ourselves such as: What am I here for? What am I to do with the rest of my life? What have I achieved? What really matters to me? Am I satisfied with what I have done with my life? Many mid-life crises occur because too much of your unique gifts and talents have been held in your light shadow, not yet lived or realized. As a result of this personality stagnation, people feel a sense of futility in which they have lost touch with their life meaning and purposes.

Those who wake up in a dark wood during their mid-life crises sometimes discover they have been living their mother or father's life and not their own. This can happen particularly when an individual is living a shame-based life in which to survive a childhood she made a shame contract with a parent or offender. Those who feel lost may also find themselves entangled in the trappings of society and the necessity of surviving within it. They then have the realization, "I haven't yet lived my own life." This feeling of being lost is particularly true of disintegrated achievers whose focus has been upon what others have told them they should do rather than upon their own unique gifts and desires.

USING HEALTH CRISES AS OPPORTUNITIES TO GROW

To heal in mid-life crisis, it is essential to either deal with our beliefs directly or we will be forced to deal with them indirectly as shadows images of negative patterns or beliefs in the physical experience of ill health. If a genuine healing is to occur during a health crises, not just curing of symptoms, a change must occur in the emotional patterns of the ill person. The healing solution to an illness is always in the conscious mind where we can make choices about beliefs concerning the nature of our being and reality. Our bodies are in a continual state of our creation, formed and made at the unconscious level in line with our beliefs about what and who we are.

It is illuminating to consider using the word "crisis" in the same way the Chinese meant it as a time of opportunity, and as the Greek root of the word for crises which means "judgement." A health crisis of a major illness such as a heart attack or a diagnosis of cancer can be an opportunity to reflect, to take responsibility and to make healthier, better choices.

Every crisis has phases of development. There is the brewing stage of a crisis. We are always given warning through hints, or intuitions, that something is wrong. Then there is the break when the crises spills into our reality and influences more and more areas of our lives. Then there is a spread of the crisis, and finally its retreat, when it is over. To cope with a health crisis, remember this too will pass; crises are times of opportunity when we can make radical shifts in our perspectives about our identities.

We can become totally different people as a result of having experienced and resolved a crisis. During a health crisis, it is essential we become wise by looking at the larger picture of our lives and what we truly value most. It may be essential to our survival to change our life-style to a less stressful one. We can then approach life in a way we would not have done before, with more respect, more delight and more appreciation for the truly valuable aspects of life. One of the things which can help during a crisis is to remember the love, not only of our family and friends, but from the spiritual forces which surround us.

STEPS TO HELP YOU HEAL
DURING A MID-LIFE CRISIS

(1) As far as possible, live **in the present moment** sensing the sensuous nature of your experiences. Instead of focusing upon your pain, focus upon other portions of your body that are at ease, paying particular attention to your immediate environment and what you enjoy about it.

(2) Imagine the best possible solution of the problem or malady you are experiencing. See it accomplished. Tell yourself now is not the time to worry. You can leave that to another time.

(3) Consider other steps to address the problem or illness.

(4) Seek out pleasure as well as discovering any shadow aspects of your problem.

(5) Free associate upon any subject you feel may influence the problem-mother, father, marriage, work, growth etc.

(6) Resist the instinctive impulse to fight/flight/ feed/or sex. Instead be quiet and encounter your illness accepting that there is an implicit order in the chaos of its presence.

(7) Ask for a deeper understanding of the implicit order beneath the chaos of your illness to emerge. Accept this implicit order offers you an opportunity to learn and grow in new ways.

SHADOW PATTERNS REVEALED BY
OUR ENNEAGRAM DRIVES

A driven life is one in which we passively surrender to our drives. This is the reverse of what we usually associate with being driven. Most of us assume that being passive means to be psychically inactive. Actually being driven by our drives is being passive. The most active response we can make when we are being driven by our drives is to pause to decide not to be driven by drives such as the drive to be right, to be special, to be safe.

Under each enneagram drive is a negative ego agenda that when taken to its extreme leads to a dead end or dark night in which there is an emptiness and despair in which new light and hope will appear if we pause to look and listen for it. I believe we are born with a primary drive already chosen by us, based upon the lessons and destiny we wish to have. To achieve our destinies, we choose parents who will help achieve the integrations of this drive and to resolve the challenges of its disintegrations related to our dark shadow work.

The enneagram is particularly useful in shadow work and holistic health because once an individual understands their enneagram type, he or she can predict accurately what their negative ego agenda is and how it acts as a filter to inhibit the psyche and prevent it from functioning freely. This function is part of the shadow because it has been repressed, denied or acted out through patterns of false identification, defensiveness and self-defeating behavior.

The enneagram drives we choose hold the secrets of our soul's code or calling. My destiny is to be a peacemaker and reformer and the great work I participate in is to in my unique way of healing to make a more peaceful, better world. This is what I am most passionate about and this destiny haunts me like a ghost with the light of the great work-the purposes I am meant to accomplish. The messages of this light shadow come through intuitions, urges, whispers, passions, dreams, impulses and desires.

The enneagram drives also hold clues as to what we need to learn so we can find a way to become whole and return to our true spirituality. As a peacemaker I need to face my resentment and anger and recognize that I do make an impact of a positive or negative nature on those around me. When I am stressed, I could become a tortoise and withdraw into dread and anxiety, but I can also choose to face my conflicts and act in honest ways.

The filter of the negative ego agenda blocks energy and can trigger illnesses. I for instance am a peacemaker with a lean on the reformer. As a peacemaker I tend to deny my anger and it has demonstrated itself through my body at various times as hypothyroidism and high blood pressure. I know that there are certain negative ego messages that continually arise that I can reject and replace with the truth.

Illness or Pain as a Dark Wood

Being in a dark wood sometime in the middle of our lives is an essential part of growing and changing. The experience of a major illness or the loss of someone you love can put you in the dark wood. You know you are in a dark wood when you feel lost and need a new direction. Instead of denying or resisting the awareness of being in the dark wood, admit you are in it; your presence in the dark wood indicates you have lost your sense of belonging. A sense of belonging is critical to finding meaning, value and enchantment in life. The dark wood is a place of chaos and confusion, but chaos always precedes and follows any change. You can then reach beyond the fear and sense of isolation, sorrow and loss for a more expanded sense of your self to emerge.

A resistance to the awareness that we are in a dark wood will keep us from eventually coming to a new sense of belonging. In the midst of the dark wood, it is important to realize our shadow-soul and the duende that holds our destiny is with us in the darkness. Part of this awareness is the recognition we need a new direction then the path we have been taking which is not right for us and has lead us to a place of despair, pain, illness and isolation. Beliefs that we are unloved or unloveable, or have to be fiercely independent, or unable to receive are obstacles to getting out of the dark wood. Our souls can then enlighten us as to what it is we can give and receive to regain our sense of belonging and value.

We have to fight to get out of the dark wood, but admitting we are in it and listening to find ways to expand and grow. There are gifts within the sorrow and darkness we can find. In earlier, primitive cultures a mid-life crisis would be honored as a time to go inward to seek the counsel of the soul. In the modern world in which soul is denied, our souls often have to speak to us through crises, tragedy, despair and illness.

If we feel the sorrow with intensity in this darkness, we can transcend it. The dark wood is not the bad place we imagine it to be when we remember to feel the remorse and compassion within our sorrow. There is always a reason that this tragedy or illness is part of our realities. In our modern world people often define themselves by physical measures of success and power rather than the quality of their love. Some people enter the dark woods of their lives during their middle shadow years and never find their way out of it. Others leave the dark woods, by finding new power, health and hope in their later years.

Those who learn the lessons of their dark shadows can approach their later-years with new vitality and integrity. They become spiritual human beings, not just human beings. They, at last, solve the problems which never go away until they have faced and transcended them to a higher level of experience. When Betty reached her forty fifth years of age, she realized that she was burnt out on her job. She earned a good wage but hated going to work. More than anything what made her know that this job was no longer right for her was the pain in her hands and arms from doing repetitive work that she found boring. Betty began to realize that she was not living the life she wished to live. She had all of the material things she could want, but she was unsatisfied and lost.

To help her find herself and get out of the dark wood, I asked Betty to make a list of ten things that would make her happy and ten things she was passionate about and then to prioritize them as to which ones were most important to her. Betty had been living with little sense of focus. Betty had many interests so she had to weed out and sort which of these interests she wished to pursue for the rest of her life. Betty had made the mistake many achievers make which was to pursue goals and interests others told her were valuable, meanwhile she had neglected her own interests.

Her physical pain forced her to slow down and nurture herself more. Betty began searching for the light in her darkness. Within this darkness, she discovered she was passionate about holistic health particularly how diet influenced people's health. She decided to take some college courses on this subject. Consequently, Betty was particularly helpful to friends and family members who suffered from diabetes and other illnesses. In the process, Betty experienced better health and less pain.

SEEKING YOUR DESTINY DURING THE DARK NIGHT OF THE SOUL

The shadow, as a face of our souls, holds the information within our soul's code and acts upon its agenda. Anything within the umbrage of the blueprint of its light destiny is something the soul nurtures, supports and co-creates. This destiny not only enhances and fulfills us but also leads us to the great work we can do to make the world better. One important way to find your destiny is through the aspect of your light shadow which has been called the daemon or duende. This is the part of our light shadow-soul which calls us to our destiny and holds the secrets of our greatness. When you feel that your daemon has misled you, this does not mean you have failed. It only means that you needed to learn something from going in the wrong direction.

To find this daemon, some go into the Dark night of their Souls where we are vulnerable to our weaknesses and strengths. Others continue to be lost for the rest of their lives. When you follow the guidance of your daemon, you are following your preferences not only your needs. The realization of these preferences can lead you to joy.

The poet Dante wrote of his own dark night in the middle of his life when he was wholly lost. When in the middle of our lives, we realize we are living a life the authorities have dictated to us- our parents, teachers, society, but not the life we would choose, then we are lost. We then need to go into the dark wood of our disappointment and sorrow. In the light of our inner guidance that is in this dark wood, we can find the secrets that free us to live our destiny. The light of this inner guidance is found in our daemon who can return to us the passion we lost during the wounding of our adolescence.

When we embrace our daemon, part of our light shadow, we live life brilliantly and regain our health. The daemon holds for us our soul's plan, a brilliant life filled with majesty and freedom. It knows who we are and what we have forgotten and denied; it is our light shadow. When we find the daemon, we can in meditation, sit and talk with it and be fully conscious of its creative passions and energies. The daemon can be impatient and pushy like a trickster if it is denied. It knows our destiny so it may thwart us when we are going in the wrong direction; it may push us to get out of situations of pain and failure, so we can discover our strength and beauty.

In James Hillman's book *The Soul's Code*, he traces the early lives of people who were later considered self-realized or geniuses to see how their genius or white shadows grew out of their private wounding and their soul's code. Hillman believes that the soul has an agenda that can be revealed to each one of us. He studied the childhood of people who later were considered self-realized or famous in some particular way to reveal how they were influenced by their soul's code and their early wounding.

Hillman believes that the soul of each of us is given a unique blueprint or calling before we are born, and an image or pattern we hope to realize during a life time on earth. This code is given to us by a soul-companion which he calls the daemon who is there to guide us to the pattern we each choose before our birth, but subsequently forgot. The daemon remembers what our soul code is and what belongs to this pattern.

Modern psychology admits we are all unique, but has no adequate explanation of this uniqueness. Hillman proposes what he calls "the acorn theory" to explain the uniqueness of each individual. This theory proposes our uniqueness is not sourced in either nurture or nature, but in the soul. According to the acorn theory, every one of us is born with what Hillman calls a soul's code, or the blueprint of what we wished to realize.

Hillman bases his psychology on Platonist teachings that believes we elect the body, the parents, the place and the circumstances most conducive to our souls' plan for us.

These teachings are consistent with those of the enneagram that say we choose our parents so we can form a reality in which this drive will come out of the unconscious into the consciousness, so we will have the power to transcend our little stories and achieve our personal great work:

(1) Each one of us is called to a destiny we have chosen that allows us to grow in our character and spirituality.
(2) By paying attention to intuitions, passions, spontaneous impulses and inner awareness, we can align our lives with its agenda or pattern.

(3) The accidents, heartaches and shocks or illnesses are there to awaken us to the pattern of our daemon and the option of fulfilling its pattern or agenda.

Hillman rebels against traditional psychology which denies the force of the soul and its faces. Other cultures regard the acorn or daemon (shadow) as the design of individual destiny. Hillman notes the core subject of psychology, the psyche or soul, is not incorporated into psychology books or studies. Hillman believes other cultures have a better sense of the mysterious force in human life than modern psychology does.

My Mid-Life Crisis

My own mid-life crises occurred when I too was unhappy with my work and felt something was missing. I had by the standards of my family succeeded by getting a safe well paid bureaucratic job as a social worker for the Veterans' Administration in Alaska.

I was a GS-11 a level to which my father understood to be successful. Meanwhile I was bored and asking my co-workers if I could practice hypnotizing them. My issue was my deep desire to have a genuine healing impact upon the lives and health of my clients. To achieve this in my own creative way, I would have to leave the bureaucratic system and go into private practice social work. My interests lay in holistic healing and in bringing imagery and music into my work.

The opportunity for a change came when my husband was transferred from Alaska to Spokane. This was a time of confusion, chaos, self-doubt, uncertainty and fear about what I should do with the rest of my life. I knew that I needed to live by water, my element to find a sense of balance. When we found a small house near Liberty Lake which we decided we needed to remodel, I knew we were home. This lake also served to bring out my poet self which has always been most attuned to my spirit and soul. It was during this time that I started to have problems with peri-menopause, low thyroid and developed a Hashimoto's goiter at my throat.

I came to understand that these maladies were directly related to my strong creative urge to speak, write and heal myself and others and to my shadow resistance for this creative expression. My body was telling me there was a need for me to be creative and to express my feelings and thoughts more. During this time, I wrote this poem describing my experiences:

The Dark Wood

My life folds before me
Like a half-used sheet of paper
I could write upon
Or throw into the fire.

I have entered Dante's dark wood
And on each tree
I read the lines of my mortality,
Where is the road out of this forest?
My bones grow lighter than a bird's.

A middle-aged woman is my guide:
she says it is time to get serious
to stop my spiral dance
and settle into myself.

I shed the lace petticoats
of my grandmother and Diamond-toothed Lil

From here on in, I'll have to travel light.
The straight road is lost,
and I climb the spider's invisible stair.

Since I have lost my travelling bag
and cannot see in the dark,
My guide gives me a new pair of eyes.
There is no insurance on these eyes,
I may lose them at any moment.
But for now, I am enchanted
With the cerulean blue sky
between the bare branches.

Like a spider, I spin out into space
from what is inside.
The thread I move upon is fragile,
but it is the only road
I know.

It had long been obvious to me I would have to find my own path and could not live with the same core beliefs or life-style my parents had lived. I had a deep longing to be a healer in a way that really changed people's lives. Becoming a healer of myself and others in a deep, true way, is the destiny I began to live during my mid-life crisis. I also had a strong impulse to come closer to nature and to express myself in poetry and prose.

What I desired most was to write about my experiences as a holistic healer.

SHADOW WORK CHAPTER SEVEN-
HEALING YOUR MID-LIFE CRISIS

1. If you are in the midst of a mid-life crisis take time to pause and reflect. Take the steps mentioned in the text and examine how you can find your true path.

2. In meditation, go into the darkness of your dark night to find your duende. Let him give you clues to find your true path.

3. What is the secret of your enneagram type that can free you from being driven?

4. Contemplate what it is that causes you to suffer. Commit to living in nonviolence and transcending this suffering by accepting those things you cannot change and and facing those things you need to recognize, own, forgive and change.

5. Write and destroy shame contracts and replace them with healthier beliefs and feelings and follow your heart's desire to free yourself.

6. Recognize the dumb, repetitive thoughts your negative ego tells you. Ask your higher self and the spiritual forces to protect you from these lies and negative thoughts and beliefs.

Chapter Eight

Healing Cancer

CANCER AS A SPECIAL HEALING ISSUE

Cancer is an immune deficiency disease that occurs when we have not dealt with shadow issues such as continual or excessive anxiety, fear, hopelessness, depression, or guilt that prevent our growth. When we suffer from continual anxiety or stress and have lost our sense of purpose or desire to live, our immune systems become suppressed, and we become vulnerable to cancer and other diseases. One of the things that keep us healthy is having a sense of purpose, hope and anticipation for our futures. When people lose their hope for their future, they lose their sense of direction and will to live. A sense of purpose and passion for life activates our immune systems to prevent us from serious illnesses such as cancer.

Ruth was a professional woman who explored with me what the messages of her numerous illnesses were; the most serious of these illnesses was abdominal cancer. There were many things in her life she "could not stomach." Ruth knew without doubt the central message of her stomach cancer was hopelessness and a lack of any reason to live: She lost her reason for living when her loving relationship with a man ended several years before. She had a strong drive to love (enneagram #2) and saw herself as a loving, spiritual person, but in the process of forgiving her lover she learned he had felt controlled and unloved by her inability to commit to him. She had previously blamed him entirely for their breakup. By facing the dark side of her disintegrated lover drive-her control and fear of being hurt by love, Ruth began to heal. She forgave herself and her lover and in the process she gradually found a new sense of purpose and meaning. She also learned how to become less controlling and more genuinely loving.

When we resist entering a new phase of our lives, as Ruth did, we are like a plant that is dying and unable to grow because it has outgrown its too small pot and is root-bound. Unless we move on to another larger place and perspective in which we can expand and stretch out our roots, we will stop growing and eventually die. There is strong evidence that hopelessness or a lack of meaning and significance in one's life lowers the functioning of the immune system.

Some of the negative emotional patterns that cause this kind of hopelessness are an emotional attitude that makes it impossible for a person to love others or nurture themselves, resentment over not receiving love and nurturing, or an emotional crisis involving a loss or death of a loved one, followed by a decision there is no meaning and significance in your life. Hopelessness and continual stress result in immune suppression. All human beings produce cancer cells regularly, but if their immune systems are healthy these cells are destroyed by their immune systems. The development of cancer therefore represents a sign that the production of immune killer Cells, T-Cells, B cells and antibodies is defective.

In his book *Spontaneous Healing*, Dr. Andrew Weil, one of the foremost authorities in holistic healing, considers cancer as needing special consideration. Unlike other illnesses that depend upon the activation of the bodies intrinsic healing mechanisms, the presence of cancer in the body, even in its earliest stages, already represents a significant failure of the immune healing system. This is true because when a detectable tumor appears, it must have escaped the normal defensive network of an individual's immune system.

Dr. Weil believes that the usual allopathic treatments for cancer radiation and chemotherapy are crude treatments that will be obsolete before long. Both treatment methods are carcogenic and work by killing cells on the assumption made by the doctors who use them that cancerous cells divide faster than normal ones. Unfortunately, that is true only for a small percentage of cancers, principally childhood cancers, leukaemias, lymphomas, testicular cancer, and a few others. The side effects of radiation and chemotherapy of damage to the immune system is less obvious and much more of a concern than the more obvious ones of loss of hair, appetite and nausea. If you have cancer, the question you have to answer is whether or not the damage done to your cancer justifies the damage done to your immune system by radiation and chemotherapy treatments.

The hope for a cure of cancer depends upon whether or not our immune systems have the potential to recognize and eliminate malignant tissue. In the future, what will be most curative for cancer are not more toxic chemotherapies, but immune therapies capable of stimulating immune systems to action. Dr Weil believes that spontaneous healing of cancer occurs but is much less common than the healing of most other diseases because the healing system has already failed if a malignant cell is able to give rise to a detectable tumor. When healing does occur it is because the immune system has been activated. He believes great care must be exercised in deciding whether or not to use toxic radiation treatments and chemotherapy because these damage the immune system and may reduce the long term possibility of healing through activation of this system.

One of the functions of the immune system is to determine the difference between the self and not self. When the immune system is dysfunctional it either fails to defend the body from what is alien to it or it attacks its own healthy body. Cancer often develops when the natural process of growth is stuck or stagnated by excessive fear, unprocessed guilt, self punishment or an inability to cope with change. On a symbolic level, the immune system corresponds to our ability to cope with the world, our level of self-confidence, or the degree to which we are defensive or defenseless. If we believe we are victimized or unhealthy by nature, those beliefs form the basis of a weak, confused identity which is reflected in a dysfunctional immune system.

The immune system protects us from invaders; it is the intricate network of players, our T-4's killer-T-cells that defend our bodies. This system roams around mainly in our blood in search of alien energies which the body needs to defend itself against. It protects us against the unknown, enemies outside in the world. On its own, the body consciousness naturally moves toward health, expression and healing. The cells of the body communicate and cooperate with each other and effectively defend us against alien carcinogens and inner stresses. However, if a negative ego pattern with its agendas is chronic or replaces the true selves wiser ones, then illness and suffering can occur. A negative ego pattern causes undue and often chronic stress upon the body.

The negative ego by defending the idealized self of society or family may act like a weak immune system that has lost contact with what is its true self. If the ego denies too much of the feelings and thoughts that are genuinely its own, it is not surprising that the immune systems is confused and weak and unable to function properly. Some people deny, devalue and do not permit anger or aggression to be expressed. Others do not permit sexuality, strong emotions, vulnerability or sexuality. Some do not permit creative expression, intellectual development or financial abundance.

The body's immune system protects it from many of the mind's negative beliefs and their related emotions, but when these stressful patterns are chronic, acute or persistent, the natural ability of the body to protect and heal itself weakens. Cancer is the second major killer of people in our western world Cancer occurs when the immune system of a body has become weak, without direction, and thus ineffective in protecting us from both outer carcinogens and inner stresses.

There are numerous forms of cancer, but all cancers cells are primitive, non-productive, alien cells that overwhelm, multiply and replace healthy ones of the healthy, vital body. Cancer may symbolically be a disease in which the non-self or false, inauthentic self gradually destroys the true, authentic one. The researcher Graham and his associates identified the typical attitude of those who acquired cancer as a deep despair and dissatisfaction about their social situation and circumstances of their life. This despairing, hopeless attitude believes if only they were a different sex, social class or had different opportunities; their life would have been different.

FIGHTING FOR AN AUTHENTIC
LIFE FREE FROM CANCER

The work of Lawrence Le Shan and researchers like Graham suggests that the symbolic core of cancer may be the presence of a false, inauthentic self as a result of not allowing the true self to feel and express itself and its true emotions, so it can become aware of them and make healthier choices. When we resist and repress our natural abilities, strengths, and our light shadows and authentic selves, we weaken our immune systems. In his **book** *You can Fight for your Life,* Lawrence Le Shan tells the stories of numerous cancer patients who were considered terminally ill until they began to focus upon and discover their true authentic selves.

One of these patients was a young man with brain cancer who had pleased his parents by becoming a lawyer, but who really wished to become a musician. When he began allowing himself to become the musician he truly wished to be, his brain cancer healed and disappeared. Lawrence Le Shan worked with a group of cancer patients who all had dire prognoses for recovery and who had been told they had a terminal illness. He found that by encouraging them to seek and discover those things which gave them a reason to live, and a future, he was able to both prolong and heal a significant number of these patients. The discovery of a passion on which they could focus such as playing the piano, studying the history of ballet, or finding a new person to love, served to give them a sense of balance and direction these cancer patients had previously lacked.

The lesser self in its efforts to be an idealized self denies socially unacceptable feelings such as their anger, hurt or fear and then becomes dominated by these emotions, instead of releasing and resolving them. When people are taught as children that only "good" thoughts can be expressed or that they can only be seen not heard, they learn to suppress their natural exuberance. As a consequence both angry and happy feelings are numbed. In the depth of these feelings could be found their identity, creativity and destiny. To feel with intensity means we cope with experiences and their related emotions with honesty, integrity and intensity, and then let them go.

HOPELESSNESS AND THE
DEVELOPMENT OF CANCER

When Lawrence Le Shan worked with cancer patients who had a terminal illness he searched for areas of their lives in which they had enthusiasm, beauty and hope. Hope is a powerful force of nature, a vessel that holds the space for our expectations and anticipations. In truth, hope emerges from and is part of soul and spirit. Hope is what initiates all of life and creative endeavors. Without hope, each of us becomes weak as individuals, and without hope, nations die.

When we feel hopeless, powerless and dispirited, our shadows hold the hope we deny. Hope is a feminine energy and in a chauvinistic world, feminine energy is seen as a weak or of lesser value, relegated to children, women and older people. Hope is then seen as the desperate and an embarrassing option, not open to real powerful people.

Our value is not determined by achievements or relationships. The loss of a job or an important relationship may provoke guilt, failure or fear of the unknown. There may also be a pattern of self-denial or denial of the truth about a situation that calls us to be more honest and expressive about our relationships to others or to our work.

Each of us comes into the world as infants with a sense of soul hope that keeps us filled with soul and spirit. As we enter adolescence we experience a wounding that causes us to lose some of our spirit. Our souls remain with us as our shadows but they too can be denied or lost. Hope then loses its meaning and with it its significance. Hope then becomes something that is devalued by the consensus reality as the desperate act of women, children and the old. Hope is an incredibly powerful force; it is a key to good health because it connects us to the future and triggers our dreams. Hopelessness and the related helplessness that comes from it, weakens the immune system and increases the risk of illnesses from all sources, particularly from cancerous growths.

CANCER AND THE SUPPRESSION OF FEELINGS

There is much debate about whether certain personality traits or patterns are more prone to certain diseases such as having a "cancer prone" or "heart disease prone" personality. Much of the evidence in support of this link between personality traits comes from the forty–year study conducted by Dr. Caroline Thomas of John Hopkins Medical School. Dr. Thomas collected large amounts of information on the psychological status of the medical students starting in the 1940's. She followed these students over the years as they got older to discover what psychological factors contributed to making them sick and later to die.

Dr. Thomas was able to correlate particular psychological characteristics and early family experiences that these doctors reported when they were young and healthy with a range of different diseases that some of them experienced over the next forty years. One of the findings of this study was there was a correlation with a lack of close relationship to parents and an ambivalent attitude toward life and human relationships that was associated with an increased likelihood of having cancer later in life.

Another study of personality patterns that are related to cancer was done by Dr. David Kissen at the University of Glasgow in Scotland on male patients with lung cancer in the late 1950's. The personal history of these men was studied before any diagnosis was made. Those patients who were later found to have lung cancer had more unhappy childhood experiences and disturbed interpersonal relationships, including the death of a parent, than did those patients who had other diagnoses. The Kissen researchers observed that as a group the men with lung cancer showed particular difficulty in expressing their emotions.

These men did not express their feelings about traumatic events, especially those that involved bonds with other people (such as marital problems or the death of a relative) Instead they denied they were feeling emotional pain and talked of their difficulties in matter-of- fact tones that seemed inappropriate to those who interviewed them. The inability to express emotions was strongly linked to mortality among the lung cancer patients in this study. Those people who had the poorest ability to express their emotions had more than four and a half times the yearly death rate as those lung cancer patients with the highest ability to express emotions. This finding held true regardless of whether or how much they smoked cigarettes.

The suppression of feelings as a precursor and possible causal factor of a "cancer prone" personality was again studied at King's College Hospital in London by Dr. Greer and Tina Morris. A large group of 150 women were given in depth psychological interviews when they were admitted to the hospital for a lump in the breast. All of these women were under the stress of not knowing whether or not the lump was cancerous. These interviews with the women and close relatives had the purpose of determining whether or not these women suppressed or expressed their feelings.

It was discovered that those who had benign outcomes in which no cancerous tumors were found had healthy modes of expression. Those who were found to have cancerous tumors had either a lifetime pattern of suppressing their feelings, or sometimes exploded with emotion, especially with anger. Of the fifty women from this group who were found to have breast cancer, those that survived after a five-year follow up were those who had a fighting spirit rather than a suppressed, hopeless or stoical attitude.

The researcher Lydia Temoshok has researched the behavioral pattern she calls Type C in patients with cancer. The core of this pattern is an inhibition of feelings, especially anger. She theorized that this type of behavior puts patients at risk for virulent forms of cancer as it weakens the immune system. It was her theory that the development of malignancies is related to a breakdown in the immune system as a result of feeling stuck in a stressful situation in which a person felt unable to flee or fight. In her research with patients having skin cancer, Temoshok found those patients who were unexpressive had faster growing, more virulent cancer. The opposite was true of those who were more expressive.

Type C personality is based upon conformity to socially acceptable behaviors, so angers or anxieties are often hidden so deeply that the cancer patient is not fully aware of their presence. To become more aware of the shadow of feelings such as anger, rage or hurt that may be denied or rejected, cancer patients can begin by asking questions such as these: "Do I permit myself to feel and express anger or hurt honestly and appropriately?" "Do I permit myself to aggressively pursue my needs and desires?" "Do I accept and express all my thoughts and feelings honestly and appropriately, not just the socially acceptable ones?"

Temoshok recognized Type C behavior could be changed by a program that encouraged emotional flexibility to help people contact their feelings, soften their defenses, and change their relationships. If only socially acceptable thoughts or feelings are allowed expression, the angry or aggressive ones are held in the body where they can lead to a feeling of stagnation and defenselessness. **Defenseless people** feel victimized, martyred and self-pitying in relationship to their personal and global world. They feel hopeless, helpless and without dreams or a future. They also lack confidence in their ability to cope with the world. The feelings most associated with defenselessness are rage and despair.

THE HEALING OF PANCREATIC CANCER

Even illnesses with grave prognoses can be healed if the unhealthy emotional and mental pattern from which they are sourced is changed. Judy was a young happily married woman with two young sons. She had been given the diagnosis of pancreatic cancer and the grim prognosis that she had as little as six weeks to live. She had been advised to get her affairs in order and to write letters of good-bye to her sons. When she came to me I gave her hope and asked her to write to her sons, but to tell them the reasons she wished to live and what it was she wished to do and be in their future together.

Judy had a strong desire to live. Together we created a healing meditation tape using buckets of magic to be poured over her pancreatic tumor. At that time, over ten years ago only a small percentage of people with this diagnosis survived. Judy was one of the survivors. The meditation tape I created for her used music and images that inspired her. In creating this tape, I used the format the Simonton's recommend in their book *Getting Well Again*, but added to it healing suggestions concerning underlying unhealthy patterns we recognized were stressful for her.

Judy's negative ego drive was to be a perfectionist. Her healings tape suggested she slow down, be present and enjoy every moment and be able to make mistakes without expecting herself to be perfect. The Simonton book is a classic text for those who wish to use guided imagery to heal themselves or others. The success that the Simonton's had is using imagery to heal cancer is real, scientifically based and needs to be given more serious attention by the conventional medical world. Those who care for cancer patients need to use all the tools available for healing including the use of imagination.

Judy had the negative ego pattern of shame; she measured herself by a yardstick of perfectionism. The healing affirmations within her tape encouraged her to be more accepting, forgiving and nurturing to herself and others. Her yardstick of perfectionism was impossible and unhealthy because it was a chronic source of anxiety and stress. Judy listened to this healing tape daily. This tape spoke to her subconscious and unconscious minds to imagine the tumor disappearing and to suggest she focus on a healthier present and future.

This healing tape replaced the relentless, impossible standards of her negative ego with more accepting, nurturing beliefs and standards. After six months of listening to this healing tape, the pancreatic tumor had shrunk to the size of a pea and this was surgically removed. Judy enjoyed her life with her family and lived to see her sons grow up and to hold a grandchild. She changed her beliefs and in the process created a life that allowed her to enjoy her life with her husband and children.

HEALING THE HOPELESSNESS OF CANCER

The power of healing cancer is in the present, but its healing lies in the hope of the future. Therapists have long focused upon what happened in the past to unravel its blockages. More important than the past is the need to imagine and move toward a more positive future. The most powerful way to heal is by changing your beliefs in the present moment through either visualization or affirmation of new healthier beliefs for as little as five minutes in a focused way. Our beliefs direct, generate and focus our feelings. The imagination of a more positive future can be the anchor which can move and motivate us to heal. Judy had to change her beliefs about who she was and to use her imagination to focus upon living with less stress and anxiety.

Judy used a guided imagery and music tape we created together using her images and music. Anyone with cancer can spend five or ten minutes a day using the power of natural hypnosis as a method of accepting desired new beliefs. All that is needed during for this time is concentration with feeling upon a visualization or belief. This new belief or visualization focuses upon the desired changes you wish to make within your body and mind. This is not a foreign process, as all of us are daily being hypnotized by our beliefs; the difference in this healing process is we choose to do it consciously and with intensity substituting healthier beliefs for those that are more limiting and stressful.

The future is the motivation for all change and growth; the future is the source of all healing. If we don't have a positive sense of the future, we won't grow and heal. When a person is willing and able to imagine a more positive future, he or she can lift out of the negative patterns of the present or past. Our future selves can clarify our identity, and either strengthen or weaken our valued self. This future self can bring us the meaning and significance that we may not have found in either our past or present.

Suppressed and repressed anger is often stuffed in an organ or in some part of the body that represents the issue the cancer symbolizes. The cancer often develops in a time period when an individual feels he or she might as well just give up because they feel such despair. It is almost as if the patient is saying it would be easier to die than to live in such a despairing, hopeless state. When a person is in a depressed state their immune system senses this and it functions at a lower level, so is not as vigilant to foreign cancerous cells developing and growing.

Anger is often so deeply repressed by those who have cancer it takes the form of anxiety or depression. One of the main sources of anxiety is undefined anger. This anger can be expressed as guilt, (anger you think you have no right to), or in depression, (anger you think you will get in trouble for) if you express it. Guilt needs to be expressed by recognizing the underlying anger beneath it and expressing that. Depression occurs when there have been many seemly insignificant incidents in which a person feels invisible or feels a powerless rage.

Many cancer patients feel victimized in their social situations; they have put up with undesirable situations and conditions for years which most people would walk away from and start anew. These patients have felt powerless, unable to change, yet are not willing to change their situation. To help heal their illness holistically, what needs to be aroused is a belief in their strength and power. Instead of looking for solutions to their issues, these cancer patients believe it is hopeless to change and grow.

HEALING THE NEGATIVE EMOTIONAL PATTERN OF PERFECTIONISM

Our beliefs about what is desirable and what is not, what is good or evil, are not separate from the condition of our bodies. Our ideas about what is valuable or not can help us become healthier or bring about disease. Our conscious beliefs about reality form our experience, including the condition of our bodies.

Suppose you believe that to be a good person, you must try to be perfect. You believe that to be spiritual, it is your duty to be as perfect as spirit is. To this end, you try to deny all imperfect thoughts and emotions, such as thoughts of anger or fear. You even deny the desires of your body as you believe these are not as pure as your thoughts. You may even know that your thoughts create your reality, so you become frightened of any mental or emotional expressions of aggression. Your fear of hurting someone else then constricts your impulses to be spontaneous, creative and mobile. Since being perfect is an impossible goal, you then are always in a state of anxiety with unrecognized fear or anger.

Being perfect implies that your goal is to become complete and then need no further development or creativity. This attitude denies the nature of spirit which is always to be expanding and growing in a creative way. Eastern and Western religions have also denied the needs and desires of the body as being inferior to those of the mind. In the process, these religions have denied and rejected the intelligence and spirit within the body that is there to cooperate with the conscious mind rather than be its adversary.

Left alone our thoughts come and go. Our feelings are innocent and when expressed honestly and appropriately have no ill effect upon our bodies. They are what they are, as rain is to the earth, or wind is to a storm. Anger has a place in our lives, and sometimes is the storm or wind that can motivate us to act or move when we need to make changes or let go of constrictive, stagnant relationships or social situations. Some people fear aggressive action because they have forgotten its positive power.

In any creative process, there is a place for the power of aggressive, dynamic action. To give birth to a child, a painting or a poem requires aggressive action and expression. When normal aggressiveness is repressed, ignored or denied for a long time, it can lead to violent action that would not have occurred if more normal aggressive actions had been allowed. The chained dog may in time become violent, and the imprisoned man can also learn to become more violent than he would have become if allowed more natural expression of his natural abilities and talents.

The wisest advice in reversing unhealthy, limiting beliefs is instead of focusing upon the cancer or illness is to change the core beliefs that underlie it. If you do not like the condition of your body, you need to change your negative beliefs A perfectionist such as Judy can focus upon expressing her feelings and thoughts, then forgiving herself for those she dislikes, and then releasing them and replacing them with healthier ones. Judy also concentrated upon seeing her immune system get stronger and stronger, and her life becoming more and more vital and filled with well being, enthusiasm and love. Limiting beliefs lower the immune system and create an environment ripe for illnesses like cancer.

THE INNER STRESS OF ANXIETY

Anxiety is often dismissed as simply a product of the fast pace of modern life. What is discounted in this dismissal is the harmful effects anxiety has upon the body, mind, and emotions of people who experience and live it. Anxiety is present whenever there are patterns of hypercritical/perfectionism, self-sacrifice/martyrdom and self esteem sought through seeking approval through outside validation rather than from inner principles.

There are a number of faces of anxiety that need to be recognized for them to be healed. Anxiety is present whenever there is undefined fear, anger, hurt or self-pity. If we refuse to recognize we are experiencing any of these emotions, we will be anxious. If we do not recognize we are afraid, we will become anxious. If we are angry at our spouses, but unable to express or recognize our anger, we will instead feel anxious.

Anxiety is also an expectation of error. It is little wonder perfectionists feel anxious because failure is not something they allow themselves to do. If they do make a mistake, which we all do, they feel anxious and have trouble forgiving themselves. If perfectionists think they are perfect, which of course is impossible, forgiveness is unnecessary. Without forgiveness of themselves and others, change and healing is impossible. A shame-based childhood sets them up for error, but does not teach them to forgive or deal with failure and mistakes which are inevitable.

Some of the sources of anxiety are the anticipation of humiliation, rejection, abandonment or betrayal, inappropriate trust of someone or thing that is untrustworthy, and unprecedented happiness, fun and joy. The joy of falling in love or being successful for some one who has not experienced this kind of love or success before, may produce a state of temporary anxiety, until they can accept their new good fortune.

High levels or norepinephrine are involved in producing the "fear response of "fight or flight" in response to a threatening stimulus. Norepinephrine is a neurotransmitter produced in the brain that signals the body instantaneously to prepare for a dangerous situation. Elevated levels of norepinephrine are associated with all the anxiety disorders and the stress response.

If the stress response is chronic and long lasting due to real or imagined threats, life is prematurely shortened by diseases such as cancer and coronary heart disease.

Anger and hurt that are undefined and unexpressed become a vague anxiety that triggers a chemical chain reaction within the body that can result in cancer, if prolonged and acute. The hypothalamus reacts to our anxiety by releasing a hormone called tryptophane, a growth hormone essential to children especially in adolescence. Tryptophane lets the body know that you need to grow. When we are anxious, our bodies respond by releasing serotonin, the purpose of which is to wake us up, to give us the mental clarity we need to solve our problems and grow.

However if this hormonal chemical chain does not get the desired effect to calm and give us peace, these hormones continue to flood our bodies and there is an excess of the growth hormones tryptophane and serotonin. These two hormones then encourage the rapid growth of cells that can be dangerous. Cancer is just such a rapid growth. It is essential therefore to process anxiety so it does not become chronic or acute.

Through the use of imagination alone, you can trigger the neurotransmitters in your brain that activate hormones and glands which release chemicals that affect physical neuropeptides and dendrites. Through the trigger of the imagination, we can activate a healing response that is more powerful than we can imagine. This healing response creates a resonance which activates the unconscious and subconscious minds to do whatever is needed to heal the body and mind. To help heal cancer, it is important to seek and use imagery or symbolism that feels comfortable and acceptable to the cancer patient. Imagery is extremely effective particularly if it is acceptable to the patient. Many cancer patients prefer neutral rather than aggressive imagery to eradicate cancerous growths. I have found the healing images of a bucket of magic, sunlight, or rainbows effective in healing cancerous tumors.

KEEPING CANCER IN REMISSION
THROUGH SELF-KNOWLEDGE

Recognizing what you truly believe about yourself is essential to health and vitality. If you want to know what you think of yourself, ask yourself what you think of others. What you think of others is what you think you are, not necessarily what you are. If you see only evil and ugliness in others, you will also focus upon what you consider evil in yourself without recognizing your own good intent. Recognize a negative image of yourself is only an opinion you have, not the truth of who you truly are. This image may be a reflection of childhood programming you need to release. If you judge people around you harshly, you will do the same to yourself.

Repressed anger in its many forms such as guilt, depression and rage when stuffed in the body is lethal. Cancer patients are often considered to be saints by others because often they put the needs of others before theirs even when they are terminally ill. Cancer is a disease of "nice people," but not necessary nice to themselves. Cancer patients heal better if they allow themselves to express all of their feelings in honest, appropriate ways.

To be healthy, we can learn to appreciate the grace and rightness of our own unique bodies and minds. We can believe in our own good health. To do this, it is important not to trust anyone who tells us that we or our feelings are evil by nature. Many people in our culture refuse to love themselves because they feel guilty when they are always comparing themselves to some idealized image of themselves. They confuse self love with selfishness. When they refuse to love themselves they become like a broken ladder with one side broken or missing.

George at the age of forty two had been free of stomach cancer for two years after undergoing chemotherapy treatments. However his immune system was low and he had other neurological difficulties such as tremors in his hands and back pain. George prided himself on not setting boundaries upon those he worked with who put many demands upon him. George was a perfectionist as an electoral engineer and preferred to do a job himself rather than be frustrated with the work of others who he believed would not do a job as well as he would. George often took on more work than he could accomplish and found himself overburdened with impossible demands he later regretted.

He felt angry at some of his co-workers who he considered undisciplined. Instead of confronting them, he numbed his feelings and denied his anger. There were many things, "he couldn't stomach" in his work place and home, but decided he would be silent. In his family of origin no one was allowed to express anger as it was considered unchristian to do so. He continued to have digestive problems and back pain in his lower back.

I asked George to focus upon his lower back and to identify what it was in his life at that time that was painful. As he did so, tears came to his eyes and he realized that he was still in a great deal of grief and hurt over his recent divorce from his wife. He had been married for twenty-five years and felt she had abandoned him when she found another man to love. He also felt his divorce settlement was unfair and he had not forgiven her for leaving him for another man.

We talked about his need to forgive her and himself by exploring why she had felt unloved by him. To forgive himself George needed to love himself more, but George believed this was being selfish, as this was what he had been taught in his Christian tradition. I explained to him that self love is the foundation upon which a healthy life is built. Unless we love ourselves, we will not know how to give and receive love without conflict and resentment. George soon began to realize that he had been neglectful as a husband because of his tendency to martyr himself for his work and pay little attention to his wife and children.

When I told him that it was important in his healing process to change his life-style and stop his pattern of seeking approval to prove he was valuable, George resisted this possibility. His greatest stress was his inner drive to continually get approval through his achievements. George's back and stomach pains and immune deficiencies improved when George was able to recognize, own and forgive himself for a pattern of sacrificing not only his family but his health.

George learned to recognize his need to express his anger honestly and appropriately so it would not be repressed in his body. He also was able to forgive his ex-wife by recognizing why she had left him to make a life of her own when he had ignored her need for love, affection and attention from him. He also was able to forgive himself and learn that he had much more value as a human being than he had previously imagined when he stopped measuring himself solely by his next achievement.

Self-Esteem and Immune Suppression

George suffered from a continual need to prove his self worth and value through his continual drive to achieve. His hidden agenda of seeking approval, or the disease to please, is a dangerous one because it depends upon constantly looking to approval from others as a source of your self-esteem. This negative ego agenda weakens the immune system and creates an environment in which various forms of cancer can develop.

Self esteem is the emotional evaluation or appraisal that each of us makes of ourselves. This value judgment is crucial to creating health because when that judgment is filled with hopelessness and despair, this attitude can lead to a bodily environment receptive to the development of cancer. Self-esteem is the cornerstone of our health because it bolsters our vitality and aliveness. Every other emotional reaction is affected by our level of self-esteem. Abraham Maslow, identified self-esteem as the fourth most important human need after survival, security and belonging. Self-esteem is related to all the other human needs and is one we cannot do without. We are constantly dealing with self-esteem issues because all our human needs are related to self-esteem.

Real self-esteem is the esteem each of us earns from ourselves through living according to the principles that determine our character which are integrity, honesty, responsibility, trust, having enjoyment, and not harming oneself or others. In the process of human development, self esteem is usually associated with our relationships with our fathers during the time we were from seven to ten years old. Our mothers are supposed to love us unconditionally, but it is our fathers that give us conditional love if we earn it.

One of the enemies of self-esteem is the negative ego pattern of suppressing thoughts and feelings by denying or discounting them and then allowing those feelings to persist in the body as anxiety, confusion and doubt. The negative ego agenda of seeking approval and worth through outside validation rather than your own character evaluation, weakens the immune system.

The man who depends upon the social status from his job can lose that when he retires. The woman who depends upon her luxury car to determine her value will lose this status when that car is stolen or destroyed. We all enjoy the approval of others for tasks well done, but if we depend upon this approval as a basis of our self-worth the foundation of our health will be undermined when we do not receive it from others. We may be particularly vulnerable during the crises of divorce, retirement or the death of a spouse.

Our bodies are a medium of learning and expression; they are continually being created. Our bodies are our most intimate feedback system, changing continually with our beliefs, thoughts and experiences. If we don't like the condition of our body, we have to first change the mental image in our mind that created this physical condition. We are not at the mercy of our unconscious minds, there is an overlap between our conscious minds and in which our unconscious becomes conscious, especially when we are in a relaxed and receptive posture. We are multidimensional people. By affirming the power and grace of our own unique selves, we have the power to heal ourselves and to suffer less and enjoy our lives more.

Eleanor Limmer M.S.W.

SHADOW WORK FOR CHAPTER
EIGHT-HEALING CANCER

(1) Make an assessment of your level of self-esteem by determining from one to ten your degree of responsibility, trust, honesty, having enjoyment, doing no harm to yourself or others. In the areas in which you are low, see if you can raise your level for instance by being more responsible or trustworthy to yourself or others.

(2) What is your level of self-love? Determine this by asking how respecting, giving, caring and trusting are you of yourself? Do you follow your own inner guidance or do you depend upon the advice or rules of others?

(3) In what situations or experiences do you feel guilty? What beliefs are related to your feelings of guilt? Recognize the origin of these beliefs in childhood and replace these beliefs with wiser, healthier ones.

(4) If you have cancer or are in remission, ask yourself how did cancer reflect my dark shadow issues? Take five to ten minutes a day affirming a healthier belief system or visualizing what a healthier pattern of behaviour would look like. What did this cancer reveal to you about the person you wish to be?

(5) How can the diagnosis of cancer become a turning point in your life in which you can give yourself permission to follow your own inner guidance and true path?

Chapter Nine

Healing Immune
Dysfunctional Diseases

*A*utoimmune diseases such as arthritis, hypothyroidism, colitis or fibromyalgia are often related to trying to obtain our self-esteem in a false way. **True self-esteem is the cornerstone of good health we earn from ourselves through acting on our ideals of honesty, responsibility, trust, integrity and doing no harm to others.** The source of our esteem needs to come from ourselves if we are to be healthy. If we try to get it from others we will soon resent and be angry at those who do not or cannot give it to us. False self-esteem leads to inappropriate, impossible and destructive hidden agendas containing dark negative egos agendas as substitutes for true self-esteem.

Ellen told me she had once suffered from Graves Disease or hyperthyroidism in which her immune system was producing too much thyroid. The traditional medical solution was unacceptable to her. This was to give her a cup of radioactive liquid to drink which would subsequently kill her thyroid. When she saw the technician dressed in protective clothing bringing this "healing potion," she could not let herself drink it. She knew that if she did drink this potion, she would have hypothyroidism and be required to take thyroid medication to compensate for the loss of her thyroid for the rest of her life.

Ellen turned to alternative medicine seeking a real, healing solution which did not destroy her body with its devastating effects.

As part of her healing process, Ellen confronted her husband concerning his affair with another woman and got a divorce. She realized that there were too many unspoken issues in their marriage. His infidelity was only the outer expression of his irresponsibility to her and their sons. The most significant of these issues was his demand that she constantly please and give to him, without any positive emotional return on his part. He considered home and family her domain and not his responsibility. Ellen's dark shadow was her negative agenda of seeking approval instead of love from her husband and her low self-esteem which depended upon his presence to survive. Her fear, dependency and low esteem allowed him to manipulate, hurt and prolong their broken marriage.

Ellen believed she needed a man in her life to survive. When Ellen resumed her professional occupation as a physical therapist she found she could function well as a single mother. When she expressed her feelings, learned to receive as well as give, developed genuine self esteem based upon her own ideals of self responsibility and integrity, her hyperthyroidism healed. To heal an autoimmune disease such as arthritis, fibromyalgia, hypo and hyperthyroidism, it is helpful for people with these autoimmune diseases to identify the beliefs that tell them to constrict or defend themselves in a defensive position against parts of themselves, the world, or others.

Then they can determine whether these beliefs are true or false. Ellen held the belief from childhood-she could never survive without a man in her life. This belief had come from her mother, and she had accepted it, but when she began to trust herself more and have more confidence in her ability to be self-supporting, she realized this belief was untrue.

There is an epidemic of autoimmune illnesses in our country that afflict 12 million Americans, three fourths of those people are women. There is a group of eighty chronic autoimmune disorders all of which share the common trait in which the immune system attacks the body's healthy functions. Some of the most common autoimmune illnesses are type 1 diabetes, rheumatoid arthritis, psoriasis, and Graves disease. Other less commonly known diseases are lupus, scleroderma and fibromyalgia. Our immune systems are supposed to be the protectors of our bodies, however in these diseases the system that is suppose to protect us is attacking us. Healing an autoimmune disease suggest we look at how our immune system reflects how defensive or defenseless we are.

One of the hidden agendas of people with autoimmune diseases and low self esteem is to try to get their value from outside themselves by pleasing others or by performing perfectly by standards made by others. When our source of self-esteem comes from others instead of ourselves, we are susceptible to autoimmune diseases, because we are then dependent upon the approval of others who may be unreliable, untrustworthy or manipulative.

AUTOIMMUNE DISEASES AND
FALSE SELF-ESTEEM

There are several ways people try to obtain their self-esteem in false ways. These are by suppressing our feelings and thoughts, by discounting the resources by which we create our reality such as imagination and desire, and by trying to get our self-esteem by outside validation rather than from within ourselves, or by refusing to have principles of honesty, integrity, trust and responsibility. To have healthy self-esteem, an individual must adhere to principles. The healthy individual has boundaries that distinguish between those people or things that are threatening, alien, or untrustworthy and those that are not. It is as if the body is saying, "Since you are not defending yourself against those people or things that threaten you, I will do it for you, by defending you in the places where you think and feel defenseless."

One of the consequences of being defensive is reflected by having an armored body. Wilhelm Reich, a famous psychiatrist, created the concept of "armoring" which is defined as the tightness of muscles used to protect ones vulnerability. An armored body occurs when someone is chronically tense, anxious and on guard. If people fear the vulnerable and openness that is necessary to be intimate with others or nature, their bodies will become defensive by blocking personal feelings to avoid self exposure.

Autoimmune diseases often mimic each other and are interrelated with symptoms of lethargy, aching muscles and joints. These diseases are not easy to diagnose or treat. Conventional drugs that treat the symptoms of these illnesses often have serious side effects such as stomach ulcers and thinning of the bones and skin.

HEALING THE BELIEFS BENEATH A DYSFUNCTIONAL IMMUNE SYSTEM DISEASE

To heal a dysfunctional immune disease, explore the beliefs you hold that cause you to feel it is a dangerous world in which you must be in control or you will not survive. Explore what beliefs you consider to be obvious that cause you to distrust your intuitions, and inner guidance. Resist the temptation to fall into the stagnation of cultural beliefs which encourage you to distrust yourself or others, feel self-pity, or believe you are a victim. Explore how emotionally inflexible you may have become by armoring your muscles in a self protective, defensive way. How does this constriction of your body prevent you from relaxing, and flowing with life? To what degree has this constriction become painful? Recognize and change whatever core beliefs you have that tell you that you are flawed and should not trust either yourself or others.

The conscious mind is the source of healing because it alone can become aware of what beliefs are destructive to you and can then choose to release these and replace them with healthier ones. Beliefs do have an electromagnetic force that directly affects the body. Recognize and own that certain beliefs and attitudes you learned and accepted as as a child helped you survive your childhood, but are no longer true or healthy. If you are unable to identify what your beliefs are ask for the help of a holistic counselor or friend who can help you bring them out of the shadows of your mind and body. By recognizing the destructiveness of these beliefs, and taking responsibility for them, you can change and heal yourself.

JANE ROBERT'S ARTHRITIS

Jane Roberts' last books reveal the dynamics of her dark shadow issues and the negative hidden agendas beneath her Rheumatoid Arthritis. Jane and her husband Robert were open to discover the source of the Rheumatoid Arthritis that finally killed Jane at the age of 55. What they together identified but were unable to eliminate completely was Jane's core beliefs in the presence of a flawed, sinful self. This sinful self protected her from any overreaches and mistakes that might be made by her more expansive, creative self, but also was at the core of her chronic rheumatoid arthritis. Jane, who was a gifted psychic, feared she would be lazy or unproductive if she did not control her spontaneous creative impulses, especially those which urged her to move and exercise her body more freely. The belief in the presence of a flawed self originated both in her childhood and from her Catholic religious training as well as a cultural climate that accepted these beliefs.

As a child, Jane was taught by her Catholic Religion that people were sinful by nature, and therefore the power or energy within her had to be strictly disciplined to protect her from being lazy, unproductive and sinful. Jane was programmed by a drive to discipline herself strictly as a way of surviving and protecting her creative abilities during an abusive childhood experiences. As a result of this negative ego programming, Jane inhibited her natural impulses to move about freely. The healing of her arthritis required that she begin to accept her innate spontaneous, magical and creative self, the very self she rejected, because she feared it might harm herself and others.

Arthritis is a complicated disease in which the body's own immune system turns on the body and damages it. Robert Butts, Jane Robert's husband and creative partner believed Jane's arthritis was ultimately sourced in the psychological conditioning she received as a child and later precipitated by the stress of the beliefs of her inner sinful self. Marie, Jane's mother was mentally and emotionally abusive to her by blaming her existence for her own arthritis and unhappiness. As a child Jane suffered from colitis, an overactive thyroid; Jane later developed arthritis and hypothyroidism in her mid-thirties.

Butts and Roberts learned much about how to heal Jane's arthritis from Seth, the channelled entity who was the source of her many books. Seth suggested to Jane she contact her sinful self and allow it to reveal to her its negative beliefs and agenda for her. In thirty eight handwritten pages, Jane's sinful self told her it believed her suffering and symptoms were necessary for her soul's growth, and her creative self needed to be restricted least she do harm to herself or others.

Seth advised Jane and Robert not to be angry or accuse her sinful self but to understand its needs and emotions and to tell it that it had been sold a bill of goods in childhood. It was therefore understandable that it felt maligned, scared, hopeless and isolated. To heal this misconception, Seth advised Jane to write out a statement of intention so her sinful self would know exactly what she wanted for her life, rather than living out its unhealthy agenda. Jane apparently did this, but still failed to focus upon her creative, magical self which would have been the antidote and natural healer of the agenda of her sinful self.

One of the helpful suggestions Seth gave Jane to accelerate her healing process can be used to help other people who are afflicted with motion-impeding illnesses. This process addresses the lesser, defensive parts of the self such as the child, adolescent or objector-protector or sinful self. This healing process begins by imagining and loving the frightened, defensive part of you as follows:

(1) Discuss the feeling of distrust for the body and its spontaneity, this part of you has. With sympathy, not disapproval, acknowledge this hidden part of yourself has objected to your movement and growth in its attempts to protect you.

(2) Explain to this part why it no longer needs to protect and defend you from yourself.

(3) Tell it your new plan, stressing it no longer needs to be **defensive,** because it is now safe for you to be free, open and expressive.

HEALING IMMUNE SYSTEM DISEASES SUCH AS FIBROMYALGIA

Betty had fibromyalgia a disease that involves pain in many places about the body. This disease is related to painful experiences and emotional trauma. Betty's trauma was related to a chronic painful relationship with her daughter she refused to resolve. Both Betty and her daughter Michele were proud of their New York toughness with which they approached each other and the world. Although they loved each other dearly, Betty refused to allow her daughter Michelle to see all the pain she carried inside when she allowed Michelle to manipulate her.

Betty showed Michelle she was just as tough and unfeeling as she was. Meanwhile Betty's feelings of anger, rage and resentment simmered underneath. Betty refused to recognize how much Michelle truly meant to her. Betty was stronger than she allowed herself to recognize. Her strength was not in her New Yorker defensive, unfeeling, toughness but in the vulnerability of her feelings, particularly her love for her daughter Michelle. When Betty allowed herself to take down her defenses and write out and express to her daughter these feelings, their relationship became better. This intimacy with Michelle was what Betty had long desired. The pain of the fibromyalgia diminished and then disappeared when Betty was able to express the hurt and love she held inside. A refusal to give and receive love can be the root cause of many illnesses.

To heal an autoimmune system disease like fibromyalgia, it is helpful to explore how your immune system reflects your defensive attitude. Then begin to replace this defensive posture with strength, courage and assertiveness. If you feel victimized, martyred, powerless and defenseless, explore what your beliefs are concerning your present situation. Realize any beliefs that say you are powerless, inherently flawed, or alone in the universe are untrue.

These beliefs may have been true in your childhood, or may be accepted by a consensus of others, or spoken by an authoritarian person, but this does not make them true. Your power is in the present. If you are presently ill recognize that your body is continually changing and if you change your present beliefs to healthier ones, you will immediately begin to heal. If you are convinced you need protection and self-pity, recognize that this feeling is an anaesthetic stopping you from feeling your real pain and take steps to say ""No" to the part of you that encourages you to numb yourself with self-pity.

Underneath the shadow of self-pity is much anger or hurt which can be dangerous to your health if you do not release it. It helps to address the part of you that overprotects you, whatever you call it-your "superego," "objector-protector" or "immune system" and tell this side of you that you appreciate what it has done to defend you from illness, but you are now strong enough to handle the situations that are not as fearful or overwhelming as you once believed.

Do take the necessary steps to take back your power. Your power is the ability and willingness to act. Since your belief precedes your reality, you need to change your beliefs about your powerlessness. Your self-image also precedes your reality, so it is necessary for you to begin to see yourself as a powerful, healthy person. Value yourself enough to learn to ask for help when you need it rather than pity. Instead of manipulating or lying to yourself or others, learn to be genuinely powerful by recognizing and owning your talents and abilities.

HEALING FALSE SELF-ESTEEM

Jennifer had chosen a career that was approved by her parents, especially her father. When she achieved this career, she thought her father and mother would be pleased. Instead of feeling successful, she hated her work. She also was deeply hurt and angry at her father when he was too busy with his third wife and family to attend her college graduation. False self-esteem is particularly unreliable because it depends on ever changing circumstances and people. If you fit into society's mould you thus get esteem, but if you are unique and different than others, you will not measure up to popular standards of what is considered worthy of esteem.

Jennifer, although young and beautiful, was physically exhausted. There was no apparent physical reason for this exhaustion because it was sourced in her shadow hidden agenda of a disease to please. To earn the approval of her parents, she competed rather than co-operated with her friends and business colleagues. In her self deception, she lost track of what mattered to her and who she wished to become. If your self-esteem depends upon the approval of your parents, a best friend or a sporty car, you may lose your friend, crash your car, and become deeply disappointed in discovering you are living the life your parents wanted for you and not your own.

True self-esteem is sourced in our relationship to our fathers because our fathers will not give it to us unconditionally and demand that we earn it. Our mothers are expected to love and esteem us unconditionally, but we have to earn the esteem of our fathers. To heal this relationship to our fathers, we can begin to think of them as individuals with all of their individual faults or strengths, not just as our fathers. To release your father to be a man, with both weaknesses and strengths, not the idealized father of your childhood, see him as a person who may not know how to love you.

It is illuminating to determine what happened to you from the ages of seven and ten or from grade two to four because this is when you can lose your determination to be powerful, and your trust in your ability to think, feel, or develop character. In meditation, you can heal your inner child by giving it the protection and guidance it was not given before. Next identify and release your false self esteem. Feel how painful false esteem is for you. Recognize, own and forgive yourself for repressing or suppressing your thoughts and feelings, and being motivated by fear, anxiety, confusion and doubt. Build your true esteem by consciously adhering to the principles of honesty, trustworthiness, responsibility and integrity.

Recognize to what extent, you seek esteem by aspiration, and intention, rather than by what you have accomplished or created. Intention is important but not as a source of self esteem. Merely intending to repay a debt is not an honest way of actually doing it. The most common way to seek false esteem is using outside validation as a source of self esteem rather than as a source of feedback, income or job well done. False self-esteem is related to the dark shadow hidden agenda of getting praise and approval from others. This way of getting esteem depends upon other peoples' approval and praise, and society's changeable estimates of what is valuable.

To the extent you accept these variable standards of false esteem; you become progressively mentally, emotionally and physically ill. You will be filled with anxiety, worry, doubt and confusion. You will feel powerless and angry at those you depend upon to give you praise and approval. Your life becomes miserable, depressed, bitter, resentful and cynical. You become physically exhausted and suffer from autoimmune diseases. Your drive to compete with others becomes insatiable. When you have real self-esteem, you live with enthusiasm and vitality. Since aliveness is essential to good health, self-esteem is essential to good health.

HEALING SCLERODERMA AND REYNAUD'S DISEASE

One of the most dramatic examples of the symbolic expression of an autoimmune disease are the way it displays underlying emotional-mental issues underlying the diseases of Scleroderma and Reynaud's disease. People with these diseases have extreme inhibition of their aggressive tendencies and as a result they become "thick skinned" with scleroderma and suffer from cold hands as in Reynaud's disease. Scleroderma is an autoimmune disease that can become life threatening when the immune system attacks inner organs and blood vessels.

Sarah, one of my clients, had both scleroderma, and Reynaud's disease. Sarah often felt an impulse to hit her husband but inhibited this impulse because she felt it inconsistent with her image of herself as a good Christian wife. She had never learned how to assert herself in a wise way because she was raised with a twin sister who did it for her. Sarah married a large, chauvinistic man who often encroached upon her kitchen in a way that she felt offensive, but she did not know how to assert and defend herself and her personal space particularly her kitchen against his intrusive behavior.

When Sarah would not defend herself, her body did it for her in a dramatic way. Sarah's fingers and feet were blue, hard and crusty. She had lost the ends of two of her fingers and looked as though she was gradually shrinking away. Her hands and feet were chronically cold. The blood was being drained from her hands and feet and at the same time the skin on her extremities was becoming thick as if to become "thick-skinned," in a defensive posture against outside attacks.

Sarah's fear of asserting herself against an oppressive, dominating husband who had replaced her oppressive father, predisposed her to armor her body in a defensive way. This conflict found its expression in pain on the left side of her head and the right side of her body, symbolizing her inhibition of her impulses to aggressively confront male, dominating people. Instead of confronting her husband John with his dominating, intrusive behavior, Sarah literally shrunk up within herself. Her body withdrew blood from her extremities prepared her for his threatened personal attacks. Since Sarah would not set boundaries for her intrusive husband through self-assertion, her body continued to react by defending her for his threats. When stressed, her body drained blood from her hands and feet and brought this blood into the vital core of her body.

Sarah said that her father was an "ogre" who believed his children should be seen but not heard. Sarah did not wish to be like her mother who was resentful and angry, but by denying her own anger, this anger expressed itself in the shadow form of her body. Sarah had difficulty setting boundaries between her and others. In her childhood, she allowed her sister to be the assertive one in making choices and setting boundaries.

To heal herself of both diseases, Sarah began to learn how to be assertive and to set boundaries for her husband and others who dominated and intruded upon her. Using imagery, we rehearsed what she could say and do to prevent others from violating her time and space. Sarah also felt she could not defend herself because she was less important than her husband. When Sarah began to have more self-esteem and an increased ability to assert her self, her symptoms began to disappear. Her hands turned pink instead of blue and she stopped shrinking. Sarah began to express her anger cleanly and no longer allowed her husband to dominate her.

LEARNING TO BE OUTRAGED
INSTEAD OF ENRAGED

Rage is intense because it accompanies a compulsion to suppress ourselves; rage closes down and constricts our aliveness and natural assertiveness. Rage most often follows an extreme loss of value or power that happens suddenly or is suddenly realized. The wife, who suddenly realizes she has given all of her power to her husband and is powerless, feels rage. Rage is much more than the intense anger we usually associate with it. Rage is sometimes quiet or loud, sometimes quick or slow in developing. Rage not only rides upon anger but also upon loneliness, sorrow, hurt, hopelessness and shame.

Rage is unacceptable in our society, so it is often denied by the individual who has it. Rage comes when we deny shame and the intense sorrow when we realize that something has occurred that cannot be undone. It also can involve a feeling of hopelessness, a loss of soul, or a loss of our identity. Every woman in our society may feel rage to a certain extent at her loss of power, as does every awakened man who realizes that in our chauvinistic society the feminine energy of his intuition, imagination and creativity has suffered by being denied by himself or others.

One of the physical symptoms that is most often associated with rage is a feeling of chronic exhaustion that sometimes leads to chronic fatigue symptom. Closely related to this feeling of exhaustion is hopelessness. Under this hopelessness is the belief there is nothing you, or anyone else can do, to improve your life. When someone retreats into a poisonous silence and feels it is useless to speech, she or he is enraged. Another symptom of rage is having emotional outbursts of feelings that are too intense for the situation involved. When anger, loneliness or shame have been held within then any seemingly inconsequential, small incident may set off a thunderstorm of rage.

A core issue for those who have autoimmune diseases is, "What am I doing with my rage?" For most people, this rage is much more than anger that is there. Rage can be compared to a wild beast or a monster within us that feeds upon our life energy and dreams. There is never enough food to appease this beast and in the process we lose our life energy and will to live.

It is an insatiable monster and the only way we can heal it is to transform it.

The monster of rage is another form of the negative ego who feeds upon the false beliefs of envy and jealousy. Jealousy is born of competition and the belief that there is a limited supply of certain things that we aren't allowed to have, because there just is not enough for you. If your jealousy is intense, your subconscious has the dark law that prevents you from having what you want. This dark law says, "I try and try, but I will never have enough of what I want."

Envy is even more pernicious than jealousy because it is born of deprivation and the belief that there may be enough out there, but I will not get it. Envy is more extreme than jealousy and more vicious because its motive is to tear down or destroy people who do have the things you desire. The energy of both jealousy and envy is a constrictive one that robs you of your power and therefore is not available to assert your genuine desires and needs in positive ways. Women who feel jealous and envious of the men around them feel rage, and thus may look for and find fault with them.

Rage is often an unconscious emotional issue, within the shadows, of those who are within the instinctive triad of the enneagram. All the three personality drives in the instinctive triad of the enneagram have problems with aggression; eights tend to act out their aggression, nines tend to deny it, and ones tend to repress it. Beneath our personality veneer, people with these enneagram drives may be suppressing or repressing an intense anger that is an insult to their fundamental integrity.

The energy that drives our rage-as well as the energy that keeps it suppressed-can be released and redirected toward more fulfilling goals when it is first recognized and then processed by expressing it in honest and appropriate ways.

To transform an enraged state of body and mind, which is a fertile environment for autoimmune disease, it is necessary first for the enraged person to become aware of their rage. By acknowledging that this shadow monster is raging havoc upon their body; the enraged person can then allow their inner monster to become outraged in a way that energizes their life instead of depletes it.

One way to do this is in meditation, to get in touch with the enraged one within and to allow it to express its outrage at the various "impossible" situations in its life it is encountering. By allowing this monster to vent its outrage, those issues then can be seen in other perspectives. Then some ideas can arise as to ways in which the energy that has been expressed in physical symptoms can find expression in other more constructive, creative ways. If meditation is not a comfortable form for you, another exercise that can be used to express your outrage is to dialogue with the monster through writing, or with the help of a counselor who is comfortable with using imagery for healing.

Another method to heal rage, envy or jealousy is to first identify who you feel jealous and envious of, and what and why you feel this way about this person. This will give you a clue about what your belief system is. Ellen felt jealous about her girl friend's ability to make friends and engage with people until she realized she too had this ability. Instead of feeling jealous or envious of her friend, I urged her to claim this potential quality within herself. Ellen knew she made friends easily. She only needed to appreciate this ability more fully and believe she also had a special talent in making and keeping intimate friendships with others.

SHADOW WORK CHAPTER NINE- HEALING
IMMUNE DYSFUNCTIONAL DISEASES

1. Why would some one who tries to get approval through the hidden agenda of pleasing others develop an autoimmune disease such as arthritis?

2. In meditation, call upon your future self who is healthy, creative and happy to give you the wisdom necessary to heal an illness.

3. If you have an autoimmune disease pause and reflect upon how defensive or defenseless you are. Rate yourself, on a scale of 1-10 daily as to how you are becoming more trusting and open with people who are trustworthy.

4. Explore and bring to consciousness what destructive beliefs may be present beneath a dysfunctional immune disease. Ask for help from others if necessary to bring these shadow beliefs into the light of your consciousness where you can deal with them in a responsible way.

5. Ask yourself what is it you feel enraged about? Express this rage as outrage in an honest and appropriate way in some constructive way.

6. Who and what do you feel envious or jealous about? Recognize how you have a potential to express these some qualities or manifest these things in your own unique way.

Chapter Ten

Healing in the Later Life Crises

Common western cultural beliefs about aging are a dark shadow hanging over each of us, as we age. Each of us can recognize and reject these beliefs and their dark shadow.

Since so many older people deny their spirituality and their souls, this is a difficult time for them. Others come out of their shadow years without facing their dark shadow or without learning its lessons and secrets, so they make the choice of staying put and waiting to die. These people have often bought into the inappropriate, impossible hidden agendas of control, a disease to please, manipulation, revenge or martyrdom.

The common belief that old age is a time of failure and deterioration is a particularly destructive one. This belief denies old people their unique power, strength and wisdom. If we allow ourselves to believe this negative script with its destructive beliefs, we then see ourselves as leftover vestiges of our former selves. To accept this dark cultural shadow is to believe as we age our hearing, sight and mental abilities will fade. If we believe this to be true, it will be true for us. A gradual loss of hearing or sight will occur only if we stop paying attention to our environment. We can choose to reject common unhealthy beliefs and trust the integrity, wisdom and value of the gifts of aging.

THE LATER LIFE CRISIS OF THE DOUBLE

Some time between our mid-fifties and early sixties, the face of our soul changes. Out of our shadow-soul emerges the face of the soul that is the Double. The Double is the face of the soul that is with us until we die. During this later-life time of the Double, this face helps us see from a deeper, more spiritual perspective to evaluate who we are. This assessment is made not by worldly accomplishments, but on the quality of our being. Are we loving, compassionate and courageous? Do we live from a sense of the deeper aspects of love? Through the eyes of our souls, our previous accomplishments, accolades, or failures are not as important as our awakening to depth of our wisdom, loving relationships and genuine spirituality. The famous psychiatrist Carl Jung would not work with people who did not have some form of spirituality after the age of fifty-five, because he did not think they would have the depth and vulnerability to become wise.

In our mid-fifties or sixties, we come to a crisis in which we look at ourselves in the mirror of life and make one of three choices. These choices are:

(1) Become the adolescent we never were and try to live out our adolescent fantasies
(2) To abandon ourselves and wait to die by becoming absorbed in monitoring our physical processes
(3) To with gratitude, admire, appreciate, and value life and to become wise by continuing to dream, expect, grow and see from a wise perspective.

Eleanor Limmer M.S.W.

THE DARK SHADOW OF COLLECTIVE
BELIEFS ABOUT AGING

If we make the first choice of trying to relive and become the idealized youth we were never meant to be, we are feeding our negative ego's fantasies and blocking our growth. The persona of adolescence has to be released if we are to be the wise elders we are meant to be. This persona prevents us from being our authentic wise Selves. There are persona masks related to work and home in the first half of life that need to be released, so we can be more flexible and expansive in the later part of life.

If people in the later-day crises try to return to their youth to recapture its ideals with its arrogance and hubris, they will be disappointed. In the later years, status and engagement in work and child rearing is no longer a primary focus. If a person enters their retirement years with an inability or unwillingness to take off their persona masks, then the possibility of illness is present.

If too much value has been placed upon those persona masks, then the shadow of illness may loom with its negative ego patterns involving anger, rage, hurt, fear and a loss of meaning. The second choice of waiting to die is a deadly one because it buys into the dark shadow beliefs of our culture concerning aging. This choice is one that prevents us from having mature dreams and from experiencing an expansion of a deeper spiritual relationship that can bring perspective and meaning to our experiences in later life.

THE TRUE VALUE OF AGING

At the time of our later day crisis, our souls ask us to do an evaluation of our lives, to assess how valuable we think we are. The soul does not judge us. We are asked to make a critical judgement of ourselves and the quality of our lives up to that time. This judgement does not depend upon the praise or approval of others, but upon our own assessment of our selves. If our evaluation is less than positive, we can forgive ourselves and choose to become wiser, more loving and better people in our later years. This self-assessment of our value is immensely important because it will determine how we view our future, present and past.

This assessment does not need to be based upon our accomplishments in the world but instead upon our achievements-those changes in our character such as in our honesty, integrity, trust, responsibility and enjoyment that come from both our failures and our accomplishments. We may have accomplished much in the way of material gain, but if it did not change our character for the better, it was not truly an achievement. The rich man who gains his riches for instance, by being dishonest, unfair and cruel to his employees has not achieved much.

Those who have successfully faced their shadow selves emerge in their mid- fifties and early sixties being wise and fulfilled. They at last, have the life they have been waiting to live. Their lives are filled with dreams, desire, power and passion. These wise elders have a mature passion for life, and an inner radiance that makes them glow. We have all known elders who seemed to glow with a sense of the wonder of their souls and spirits. They have become wise, and they live with a sense of fulfillment and wholeness.

OUR REFLECTION OF OURSELVES

We are never without our souls. When the Double face of the soul emerges out of the shadow, it helps us assess what really matters from a wiser perspective. We can then start looking at ourselves to discover who we truly are. We are a reflection of our souls which is both within us in our bodies and outside of us. During our later years, it is valuable in meditation to visualize both the temple of our souls and to personify the soul as a living usually feminine person who can speak to us and comfort us. This of course is a rendition of our souls which will change as we do and helps us sense the feeling our soul has for us. When I first visualized my soul she looked like a beautiful magazine model, but as I grew more comfortable with her presence, this personification spontaneously changed to take on the face of a more mature motherly woman with an adoring attitude. The message to me was that my soul admired and adored me as a proud mother would. In time, she became more approachable for me and also someone who I could depend upon and speak to when I needed advice or help.

At the time of the Double, what matters to us can change. Through the eyes of our souls we can get a truer perspective of what truly matters to us. This reflection extends to the end of our lives and makes it possible for us to see ourselves and assess who we are.

The soul is a slower more feminine energy than our spirits. Our spirits can be dulled and weakened when our hopes are blocked or when we settle for less than we can become. In the depths of despair, depression or grief, we can be touched by the light of soul that is always there to give us new hope and light. Our spirits are the part of us that are searching for the divine love and energy that is found in the depths of soul.

After Jack retired he noticed that he began to appreciate his wife Joan in a deeper way; he saw her as more beautiful in her own unique ways. Instead of forcing himself to go after old hopes and projects that did not seem to be succeeding, he extracted their mattering and allowed himself to be void of mattering for a time. Life became less stressful when he refused to force himself to go after material things that no longer were valuable to him. Jack held the space for genuine matters of value to arise.

There is a paradox of hope which is the principle since hope is colored and tainted by our old level of spirit with all its old disappointments and failures, to revive our hope we need to give up our old hopes, not to be hopeless, but to be void of hope to allow new hope to arise. Giving up our old hopes allows us to receive other fresher and more vital ones to emerge. These may be the same dreams and desires, but coming to us from different energies, with fresher ideas and newer plans.

REJUVENATING OUR SPIRITS

The qualities of a soul and spirit filled elders are also the means of becoming one. Our spirits are fast, masculine energies that can be weakened or lost during times of disappointment or failure. Our spirits are always searching for the divine love that is found within the depths of our souls. Often we believe that we can satisfy ourselves and find fulfillment through things out in the world-degrees, accolades, houses, boats, or expensive cars. In our later years, we can truly get it that these things do not truly satisfy our spirits, Our spirits may wake up in the dark wood of middle age or illness and realize they are lost. A shift of perspective and new insight can then occur in which our value can come through our state of being by going inward to reconnect with our souls and spirits.

It is essential for many people to stop, get away, and take time to rejuvenate and feel the presence of their spirits by owning any one of its qualities with intensity; these qualities are **being powerful, free, good, valuable and enough**. George was a person who was always dispersing his spirit by denying his value or giving it away to his negative ego, or by depending on others to give him a sense of his value.

To revive his spirit George recalled times when he felt powerful and allowed himself to intensely feel and indentify with that feeling again, not only by feeling powerful, but knowing,

"I am powerful." By feeling and breathing in its presence, he brought it in and contained it within his body. Then he was revitalized. George had to also face the shame of his pattern of indebtedness and to forgive himself. To heal this shame he sat with his soul feeling his remorse and asking help to lift the shame of his quiet judgments and arrogance which were the source of his shame. With the help of his soul and higher self, he could then forgive himself and be free of his shame.

The transformation which can occur when we emerge from the shadow year can be considered a metamorphosis, a change of form analogous to the one a larvae undergoes after it emerges from a cocoon. If we have chosen and lived wisely, after the mid-life years are over at the age of 55-62 years, we may have the same body form but we can live with the full realization of ourselves not only as a human being, but as a spiritual-human being. In meeting and incorporating the lessons of our shadows both dark and light, then we have gathered those elements previously missing or transformed. One of the signs of this transformation is a sense of wonder, wisdom, wholeness and self-actualization.

To see through the eyes of one's soul is to be wise, not in a worldly sense, but in a spiritual one. The later years of life can be one of the most creative, valuable times of our lives. The growth that can occur during these later years can be compared to those that occur during childhood or adolescence because of the expansion of psychic, spiritual and intuitive abilities possible. It is possible to meet these years with a joyful affirmation of our experiences. Since our minds are no longer specialized in certain areas of work, our psyches are free to be more balanced and not restricted to certain areas of focus. The conscious mind is then better able to incorporate and to assimilate its unconscious contents and expanded states of consciousness are possible.

In these more expanded states of mind, chemical and hormonal changes trigger states of consciousness that transcend ordinary time-space orientations. During these experiences, body and mind operate together in more integrated, healthier ways. These expanded states also allow for an enhanced appreciation of all that is experienced. The beauty of a sunset or the face of a grandchild can be fully appreciated. These are some of positive beliefs concerning aging that can be antidotes to the common, negative ones in our western culture:

(1) I am growing in wisdom as I age.
(2) I grow in self understanding which brings me more and more peace.
(3) My senses are sharper as I am more appreciative of all I encounter.
(4) Aging gives me the opportunity to touch my immortality.
(5) Since I am rich in years, I have wisdom to teach and share with others.
(6) This is the most creative time of my life, if I allow it to be so.
(7) I am able to integrate my conscious and unconscious minds to create more.
(8) I am a valuable part of the universe and have much to give.

MY LATER-LIFE CRISIS

In my seventies, I faced the destructive societal beliefs that devalued me as an elder. These consensus beliefs reinforced my own negative egos' persistent lies that told me, "I didn't matter." This assault of negativity has to be dealt with in the same way you would fight any enemy. I denied it and remembered the many times I had succeeded in healing and helping others in various ways. I told my subconscious, "I matter and so does my work." The issue of my significance was at the heart of my childhood pain. My negative ego pattern always includes the message that neither I nor my creative endeavors really are significant, so do not matter. The delusion of insignificance is also present when I am experiencing a disintegration of my enneagram drive of the peacemaker.

In my elder years I approached the issue of mattering from a new deeper perspective that looked inward with the help of my Double-Soul for my worth, rather than outward. I express this best in the following poem dedicated to my friend Ed Tyler:

The 11th Hour

Our cells chime out their connections
to the perceptions from our centers
streaming out the secrets they hold
once hidden from us
in the most apparent places,
the twist of an arm, the ache of a heart,
the bend of a knee, clear as the nose
on our faces, no longer front page news
just information, messages we might
not wish to know, but now here.

A mirror we hold up to our faces
in which we could see our wrinkles
as ancient relics of a life well lived
or sunken ruins of judgment and despair.

It is all there in our perceptions,
how we view the cup we are given.
Is it a precious gift, or not enough to satisfy?
Is it golden leaves of autumn,
or the grin of a skeleton's skull?

As we wonder where that woman
or man we used to be has gone,
we can look deeper into our faces,
and see in our old eyes at last
the face of wisdom smiling back at us,
with more compassion, kindness
and honesty than we have ever known,
finally accepting our timeless minds,
the grace of our eternity,
the purity of a wiser vision.

The acceptance of my significance has been essential to **feeling fulfilled. In this significance is the meaning and value I create or allowed to be.** What locks up and prevents my acceptance of my significance is a lack of acceptance of my mistakes. Any creative endeavor I undertook required me to make mistakes and forgive myself for them. During this time, I wrote the script of a musical called **Return of the Great Round** about the Merlin-Arthur legend transcending time to help save a sacred grove of redwood trees from destruction. This musical has not yet been produced and could thus be considered a failure, yet in the process of writing it, I achieved much because it gave me great pleasure and a truer sense of who I am and can be.

As part of the later life crises, it is necessary to take time to assess our lives using a process of good judgement that uses a different perspective than what the world does to measure our achievements. From this perspective, we can discern the difference between our accomplishments and our genuine achievements. An accomplishment is the value given by purely physical measures of influence, money or titles. This can be distinguished from achievements that may come when the victory may not be tangible, but is a victory of character because in the process of achieving it is revealed to us the strength of our character, who we really are. These achievements can come from failures as well as accomplishments and are crafted out of our love, authority and freedom. We can fail at accomplishing some particular goal, but in the process learn who we really are or are not.

In later life, we can unite with the parts of ourselves we are missing that we denied or discarded. These parts of us were held for us within our shadow self until we were ready to claim them. We can become wise elders who embody our souls and spirits fully.

In my later years, I realize that my identity is much more than my roles as a healer, poet, writer, wife, mother or grandmother. These are all roles that enrich my life, but what I truly am is found more in my uniqueness with its qualities of compassion and understanding that I bring by my mere presence. I have grown wiser as I age, my deeper understanding has brought me a peace of mind I did not know earlier, I truly feel that I assess my environment better now than I did in the past, and I trust the poet within me more. My poet self has always seen in a more appreciative way than the rest of me. My eyesight has actually improved as I have aged.

In my seventies, I fell twice once on a wet sidewalk in Seattle and another time in a creek while walking through the woods. Both accidents caused me to break my lower left arm and wrist. I knew these accidents were not random events; they carried with them messages which could help me grow. I knew problems related to the wrists were second chakra issues related to either pleasure or creativity in all its forms. So I asked myself where I needed to enjoy myself to be more balanced on my feminine left side, and to allow more pleasure of creativity and enjoyment. I began to enjoy myself more and to realize intuitively with the eyes of my soul, I was enough and valuable just as I am.

These accidents forced me to take the time to look at my life with more intensity. One of the messages of these broken left arm and wrist were my need to fully appreciate and **know** that I was loved by my husband Don, after fifty years of marriage, and to fully appreciate his love and his devotion to me. Since I was in full arm castes, I had to depend upon him to dress, bath, and drive. Don did this service for me in a kind generous way and this helped me to feel and receive the love he willingly gave me. I felt his love more fully and receive it more completely. These unfortunate incidents made me know acutely how much I was loved and love.

I also began a new creative period that was related to my illness imposed solitude. There is an important part of me that is a healer. Often to grow, a healer has to experience his or her own healing process more deeply. When one caste was being removed from my arm I felt pain and discomfort; my daughter, Leah at this time was driving an automobile on the other side of town also felt pain and discomfort in her left arm. The close loving relationship between us allowed this empathetic, nonlocal experience. Leah had no conscious knowledge that I was having the caste removed from my arm, until later. We all are connected in mysterious ways especially to those we love.

ENCHANTED AGING

Enchantment is a key to creating a healthy and happy later life. Wise elders are distinguished by their ability to not be afraid to go into the chaos around them to seek out resolutions to problems by awakening what is exceptional and individual in themselves and others. Then they are challenged not to settle or be complacent, but to lead by using their wisdom and unique talents. As elders, we have more opportunities to be enchanted by everyday experiences, by the depth and richness of our understanding of ordinary experiences and events.

When elders are living an enchanted life, they feel connected to all things and are aware that everything is alive, connected, wondrous and conscious. They know they belong and matter to the world, even if this is only to a small group of friends and family. Wise elders know that their lives are structured around a foundation of meaning and purpose that emerges out of the experiences of their lives. Although we live in a world that is disenchanted by science and many traditional beliefs, we as elders can wait upon the chaos around us to find the implicit order and meaning within it that can feed our souls by the light and beauty it brings us. This order can come from the beauty of a grandchild's face or the thrill of observing the grace of a deer visiting our neighborhood. The enchantment of knowing we are at the right place and time can also come from caring for a sick neighbor or troubled friend.

Enchantment is based on the belief that we belong; we are connected and are not separate. For elders who experience the grief of the loss of friends and family this means we maintain a quality of intensity in which we allow ourselves time to grieve, to feel that grief fully, and then let it go. When illness comes, instead of resisting it as a message, we can consider it a challenge to face and pause to listen for it to reveal the implicit order beneath it, knowing there is something we are meant to learn through this experience however painful, knowing we can learn and transcend whatever lesson it brings us.

The poet part of me has always been way ahead of the rest of me, because that part of me experiences with a depth of feeling and intuitive direct knowledge. The poet in me is enchanted with experiences that the logical self tries to follow like a dull companion. Now that I am in my seventies, the poet has grown stronger and more confident. I have more and more surrendered up my "sense of separation." This does not mean I have given up my individuality or grown soft, mushy or sentiment in my old age; I have grown more individualistic than ever, with more trust in my creative impulses and insights.

THE CHOICE TO RESIST THE
ENTROPY OF AGING

We all have a choice of whether we wish to hold on to the common negative beliefs about aging or to grow into a more mature, healthy and enchanted wisdom. Choice can and does trump biology, genetics and the process of entropy. We need only to study the aged people of long living population to notice the joy of life, the purpose and passion for life that is an essential ingredient to living well and long.

To live a passionate, long life of celebration and creativity, we can look at the example of certain artists such as Pueblo Picasso, Matisse and Georgia O'Keefe. Each of these artists lived long lives rich in intensity, a sense of rightness, and purpose in a passionate way. Each lived with intensity in the moment, paid attention to detail, looked more deeply, and let go of the moment when it passed. These artists were constantly growing and pursuing what triggered their passions in relationships, art, spirituality and nature. Each one allowed their lives to flow with imagination, creativity, and passion for their work and art.

One of the essential ingredients of overcoming an entropy while aging is to focus upon what it is that you are passionate about and accept the need to pursue that by acting upon where it leads you. **To be passionate is to have boundless love, unbridled enthusiasm, and insatiable longing.** Pursuing your passions is a successful way to prevent you from living unhealthy, cultural templates that are associated with aging.

One of these consensus beliefs says elders should retire and be comfortable; this precludes a bold, daring approach inherent in genuine self realization. This choice is one that values security and comfort above seeking to grow and stretch to be all you can be.

It is essential to reject the shadow societal templates that devalue elders and the gifts of wisdom and spirituality they embody. These beliefs are destructive because they are vampires of energy. These shadow beliefs encourage seniors to use the measuring devices of their youth to evaluate themselves. Our bodies will get old and entropy, unless we choose vitality and growth. Negentropy reverses and postpones entropy.

Negentropy depends upon the mastery and artistry of our spirituality; this is a genuine partnership with God/Goddess All there Is. This spirituality depends upon a living, genuine partnership and relationship that is right for you. This vibrant, living spirituality, allows us to become wise in a fluid way that is continually changing and growing. The process of entropy or decline of the body can be slowed or reversed through a process of conscious choice that acknowledges the dynamic interaction of body and mind. Embodying spirit is not just an abstract concept because being spirited means you have certain qualities such as enthusiasm, wonder and dynamic energy.

THE CHALLENGE OF ILLNESS IN LATER-LIFE

As we age, unresolved issues take on more acute forms, especially those issues that are expressed in illness. If we are addicted to blame, control, feeling sorry for ourselves, or being a victim or martyr, these issues are likely to be manifested in illness. Betty had always blamed her mother for her own unhappiness and weakness. As a result, she stuffed her anger at her mother in her left hip. In her sixties, her hip deteriorated to the point she had to use a cane. She realized if she did not heal her toxic anger she could be confined to a wheelchair in her seventies.

Betty began healing herself by realizing, owning and forgiving her mother. She realized the reason her mother was unable to love her was she feared loving and being dependent upon someone who might leave her. She realized that like her mother she feared receiving love and felt she was weak in the face of oppressive people like her father. By understanding why her mother was unable to love her in an unconditional way, Betty was able to forgive her and let go of her anger.

GROWING DURING A TERMINAL ILLNESS

The experience of an illness may bring us to the place of being the wise fool who is learning more life lessons and becoming wiser in the process. During an illness our unconscious may become more conscious; our hidden agendas and shadow issues may become apparent. These issues are the emotional patterns of sorrow, rage, fear, anger or hurt lie beneath an illness.

At the age of seventy, Joan was diagnosed with metastasized cancer of the breast. There was much sorrow and pain in Joan's life. Joan's sorrow was around the failure of her marriage. She believed her dysfunctional family had been caused by the lack of support from her ex-husband and his inability to parent their delinquent son. To forgive her ex-husband, she asked herself why he had acted the way he did and she could see that he had a low sense of esteem which made him irresponsible and negligent to her and her children. In the process of healing her sorrow, Joan realized she had married a man who was egocentric and neglectful like her mother.

Joan realized that she had associated love with suffering. She recognized how her choice of a spouse and her desire for a happy family had been thwarted by her early experiences of the pain of love. Joan forgave her mother for loving her in a conditional way that often left her lonely and confused. Love in her family of birth was often mixed with disapproval and bitterness. As an only child, Joan often felt like an outsider in the love relationship between her parents. Since love was painful, her hidden agenda was to please and get approval rather than love from others.

Joan listened daily to a healing meditation tape, we created together, which used imagery to heal her cancer. She forgave herself and the others who had contributed to her sorrow and despair. She lived eight years after her cancer reappeared, twice as long as usually expected for this diagnosis. During this time, she did the mental, emotional and spiritual work she needed to do. She travelled, painted and enjoyed her last years. Joan died peacefully at seventy-eight, surrounded by many friends and family members who celebrated both her life and death.

CREATING ETERNAL FUTURES

We are multidimensional, eternal beings. Each one of our consciousnesses lives after our deaths. We are not our brains or bodies, although we find creative expression through them during our physical life time. Without a sense of the eternal future or timeless vision, particularly at the time of the Double, around the age of fifty five to sixty years of age, we can become lost and anxious. One of the reasons people die prematurely is they have no sense of their future. Without hope in the future, there is no motivation to live or heal. To truly understand the future, it is necessary to accept the reality that you do have a future self who is not a fantasy, but can be a freer, truer sense of your self.

This future self is living the destiny we design. The unconscious mind can and frequently does transcend the limitations of time and space. Through the images of our dreams and bodies it presents us with shadow images we need to face to be whole. The unconscious also gives us hints that there is an after life that we will participate in the future after our deaths. Carl Jung, the great psychiatrist advocated a belief in immortality when he discussed the need to face our death as we age. Jung believed that the decisive question that each of us needs to ask and answer is: **Am I related to something infinite?** If we know we have a personal relationship to the infinite, we can easily avoid focusing on material things of lesser value. Jung taught and believed that we are worthy in our realization of our unique, essential embodiment of spirit and soul.

During his mid-seventies in 1944, Carl Jung was very ill and near death after suffering a heart attack. He later wrote in his autobiography about what he described as his visions during this illness. In one of these visions, he was out of his body above the earth looking out at the earth from an expansive view in which he could see several continents. The spirit of his doctor visited him in one of these visions telling him that there was a protest against him leaving earth and he needed to return. He did so with much emotional resistance. Jung described the feeling he had during this experience as an "eternal" one of a timeless, non-temporal state in which present, past and future felt to him as one and a concrete whole.

As one ages, it is a wise choice to view your eventual death without fear through an awareness of your continuity in the after life. Jung believed there were hints that such an after life existed given us through our dreams, synchronicities and near death experiences of others. A common resistance to intimacy with your future is the belief that the future is our reward for fixing and perfecting our present and past. Many people resist their futures by assuming their future is something other people or God will give them. They do not seek their future because they feel they might miss the big one someone will give them. What is lost in their resistances is clarity of mind and singularity of will.

One way to have a better relationship to your future, is in meditation, sit with your higher self and your future self and tell them what it is you want in your future, what scares you about what you want, and what your resistances are to having that future. The future allows us to heal and gives us the opportunity to change. By nurturing our imaginations and making that future come alive through exploring the options open to us, we create our futures. The uncertainty of the future can be a springboard to find fulfillment and to overcome our fears.

Our future self can reveal to us the more real, healthier self we can become. It is therefore necessary periodically to in meditation to sit down with your higher self or future self, the one who is more than you now are, to ask important questions, such as:

> "What do you know about my future?
> "What is missing from my sense of my future?"
> "What belief or blockage stands in the way of my
> dream to....?"

If we understand and feel that we are linked with the infinite in the living of our lives, our desires and attitudes change. To have a healthy body, we need to have expectations which are composed of both hope and anticipation of a positive future in which we live fully until and after our deaths. The level of our expectations has a direct physical effect upon our bodies. Our expectations or lack of them effects the electrolytes and salts levels in our bodies-particularly the levels of calcium, magnesium, potassium and sodium. When people experience a tragedy such as an earthquake, fire, or the loss of a loved one, they may have a sudden drop in the level of their electrolytes because of their lowered expectation levels. Where there is a low expectation level, the immune system is also compromised.

Through an awareness of our unconscious in dreams and bodily symbolism we experience ourselves both as both eternal and mortal. We can expand our hope and expectations of what is possible for us. Low expectations lead to a hopelessness and despair which can compromise the immune system and give viruses and malignancies the opportunity to grow. Research shows that cancer patients who have a high level of expectancy have a better chance of recovery than those who are hopeless. As we age, we can more and more have a feeling of the expansiveness and boundlessness of the infinite in our relationships and spirituality.

Expectation is the product of hope and anticipation. If we refuse to vision, dream or expect, we will replace this lack with something less positive such as cynicism, anxiety or self-doubt. When we replace expectation with anxiety, we have an internal stress reaction that can damage the internal organs such as the thyroid, heart, brain, liver and pancreas. Quantum physics teaches us that our expectations define our reality. On a molecular level, reality is defined by our expectations. Whether we live a happy life or a sad one in our latter years is dependent upon what we expect. If we expect that we will be separate and alone in the world, our fears will in time bring us this reality.

THE CHOICE TO BECOME WISE

If we choose in old age to become wise, we can find the fulfillment that comes with surrendering the illusion of separation. Then we can remember we are part of the whole. Balance in our latter years comes when we remember we are not separate from the water, sky and land; we are connected to everyone and thing. There are many reasons why people resist or find it difficult to become wise in today's world. One of the biggest obstacles to becoming wise is a lack of genuine spirituality. In our secular world there is therefore no room for wisdom. It is impossible to be wise without a genuine spirituality. What many call wisdom is really cynicism, control, fear or anxiety.

Eleanor Limmer M.S.W.

Another reason, wisdom is impossible for many is that wisdom is not part of the consensus reality which incorporates male chauvinism. Wisdom is a feminine energy; it is not part of most intellectual or academic pursuits because it does not depend upon the past; its focuses on the present and the future. To become wise, we must reject chauvinistic values and ideas which devalue all things feminine, including women. Wisdom incorporates the present, and the future, and the values of feminine energy such as imagination, conception, feeling, enchantment and intuitive knowing.

We do not have to wait until we are in the later-life crisis to become wise. We can become wise at any age if we see through the perspective of wisdom which is the lens with which we can better see the Creator. Wisdom is not a nebulous concept. It has certain important attributes that can be learned. We can become wise by following certain characteristics of a wise person. According to Lazaris these attitudes are these:

(1) You look at the bigger picture without losing sight of the current picture.
(2) You go beyond logic and reason without losing sight of logic and reason.
(3) You go beyond the rational and intellectual without losing sight of the rational.
(4) Wise people are more concerned with where they are going rather than where they have been.
(5) Wise people are more concerned with what something will lead to than what they can now prove.
(6) Wise people look at situations for what they can learn rather than for what they can reaffirm or already know.
(7) Wise people have the ability to take symbols and turn them into metaphors and from these metaphors find meaning and create significance and value.

WRITING A HEALTHY OLD AGE SCRIPT

Everyone has an old age script whether or not we are conscious of it. This script specifies how long an individual will live, and the quality of life he or she expects. Old age can be an exciting, fulfilling time, if we have positive expectations as part of our script. If you expect little or a negative experience in old age, this is what you get. Having low expectations sets you up for psychical and emotional poor health.

Old-age is the time when each of us can look at the story of our lives and decide to change it if we don't like what we see. When Denise was fifty-eight, some health problems triggered her desire to explore how she could be more healthy. Denise had chronic insomnia, occasional dizziness, and Reynaud's disease. She was the designated worrier of her biological and work family. Somehow she had tied responsibility with the need to worry. When we explored the common denominator of all her diseases what we discovered was she had two hidden agendas, the need to control and worry about a certain group of people and the need to get their approval and fix them. Under this agenda were quiet judgments and arrogance.

Instead of focusing upon her own life, Denise focused upon fixing her fellow workers and family members. With **symbiotic guilt**, Denise tried to fix, and care for her fellow workers instead of herself. Denise had the hidden agenda of the pleaser to get approval and to control those around her. She did this with symbiotic guilt. **Symbiotic guilt is unhealthy because it depends upon getting your sense of belonging by focusing upon and getting approval from and fixing others**.

To heal, Denise needed to assert her own needs, set boundaries for herself, and **forgive herself** for thinking she had to fix others to belong. Denise recognized that her role of a person with the hidden agenda **getting approval from others**

was not only unhealthy, but also impossible, inappropriate, and destructive. Denise never expected to receive love unless she gave first to others. This form of guilt requires that we ask our spiritual forces to help us release our guilt through forgiveness of ourselves and others. Denise gradually learned to receive, as well as to give love. She forgave herself for the resentment and anger she inevitably felt when she would not allow herself to be loved.

Denise had the enneagram shadow error of a safety-security personality #6 of anxiety and worry by depending upon other's approval for her security and worth. There is a shadow secret that illuminates the darkness of the unhealthy, disintegration of this drive. This secret is she could face and overcome fear without depending on the authority of others. Denise could ask her spiritual forces to heal the shame of a guilt and belief she could only belong, if and when she pleased and helped others.

SHADOW SECRETS THAT FREE US FROM THE DISINTEGRATION OF ENNEAGRAM DRIVES

These secrets can free us from the **shadow disintegrations** of our drives:

(1) **Reformers** are wrong in thinking they just need to follow rules given them by authority figures to be perfect and everything will be fine. This demand for perfection leads to stagnation, anger and self-righteousness.

(2) **Lovers** can learn that it does not work to find a special powerful other one to get their power and value.

(3) **Achievers** can learn that their value is not based upon achievement. It is a lie to believe they are only as good as their last achievement.

(4) **Seekers of the Creative** can learn they are not exceptional in having flaws that need to be corrected before they can be valuable, loved or worthy.

(5) **Thinkers** can learn that they are not going to be happy when they know everything. There is always something more to know.

(6) **Safety-Security Seekers** can learn they can face fear without depending upon the authority of others.

(7) **Adventurers** can learn they cannot outrun their pain through addictions, possessions or more experiences. They can transcend their pain only by being courageous enough to fully experience and know it.

(8) **Leaders** can learn that though life is an illusion, they do not make the rules, nor can they control other people. They can learn it is not a weakness to be empathetic and dependent on other people.

(9) **Peacemakers** can learn it is wrong to think they do not matter. Their lives matter and have the meaning and significance they can discover. By finding what matters to them they can find their autonomy.

Dark shadow beliefs are based upon fear, anger and low expectations. These beliefs can be replaced by beliefs that empower us with the knowledge that we are already loved, valued and powerful. Low expectations create a low level of health and vitality.

A later-life script includes all the ways we believe we will end our lives in joy, fulfillment and good health or in misery, boredom and increasing infirmity and poor health. Part of this script is the age when we intend to die. Some people cannot accept old age at all and choose to die at a relatively young age because of their fear of aging.

The later-life script is not written in stone and can be renegotiated as you age. For instance, if you reach the age of ninety four, the age you have decided to die, and at that age find you have some projects or issues unresolved and would like to live a few more years, you can then make a new choice to live six more years to the age of one hundred. This script includes how you want to grow-mentally, emotionally and spiritually. It also includes your expectations of yourself, and how you wish to transcend, or heal issues that need healing.

Writing a later-life script requires honesty to recognise how you can use your strengths and minimize your weaknesses. Writing this script challenges you to make wise choices so you can use the time you have left to the greatest advantage. This script calls upon you to take care of unfinished business and to reinvent yourself with a freer, more spiritual foundation by asking yourself:

(1) What dream or dreams for myself do I wish to complete?

(2) What do I want to learn or know before I die?

(3) How do I wish to grow spiritually? Who and what do I need to let go of and forgive so I can die peacefully?

(4) What special gift do I have for the world I have not yet given? What talent or ability have I not yet fully realized?

(5) What do I know I am capable of creating before I die?

(6) With what person or people do I wish to have more love and intimacy?

(7) What kind of life-style would be most satisfying to me in my later-life? Do I prefer a meditative, active or adventurous life-style?

(8) What activities satisfy and make me most happy and fulfilled?

(9) What has been missing or deficient in my life so far? What has been over-emphasized and could be reduced?

If we follow our dreams during this crisis, we can become our truest self, the wise fool who has the courage to trust life. The decisions we make during your later-life crisis will be reflected in the quality of your life in old age. If we decide, for instance, we will return to our youth-its hubris and passion, we may experience senility during our old age. This senility may not develop, however until we are ten or twenty years older.

The Dark and Light Shadow Issues of Longevity

One of the most common dark shadow issues is the belief and its accompanying fear that we are only physical beings; the assumptions related to this belief are when our bodies die our consciousnesses die with them, and we are annihilated and suffer the loss of everything we are or have been. This is a one-dimensional attitude that measures the value of life by the standard of youthfulness and the length of our life-span. Death is seen as a failure in this system. This attitude often leads to a driven, controlling, dominating attitude toward the body. Health regimes of exercise and diet are viewed as maintaining youthfulness, rather than as ways of nurturing the body. This one-dimensional attitude needs to be transcended if we are to be healthy and wise in our later years.

There is a lighter, healthier system of thought concerning aging and longevity which allows for a richer, wiser perspective. This perspective truly appreciates the depth and richness that comes with gaining wisdom through experiences and growth. Instead of seeing aging as a negative thing, this perspective recognizes the value of finding a depth and wisdom that can come only with experience. This perspective sees life as a continual adventure that can continually renew itself and find new areas of expectation, excitement, enthusiasm and adventure. From this perspective, the body is nurtured and well used but never driven or controlled.

There is both a negative and a positive side to longevity. The negative side rests in the common attitude which says we are just bodies. From this viewpoint, the measure of your value is the condition of your body. It is based upon cultural standards that value youth over old age with the belief we physically deteriorate and finally lose everything at death. The only path this recommends is a domination of the body. To release this negativity, it is necessary to reject its standards and refuse to play its game.

Beyond this consensus system of thought is a more positive one that sees life as a continual adventure full of enjoyment and possibilities for growth because you can create it this way. This attitude sees body, mind and spirit as working together to create the future of adventure and growth.

To live long, it is important to dismantle any time-bombs in your death or old age script and to write a new script that transcends these death traps. One of these death traps is the belief that because members of your family always died young, you will do the same. Another death-trap is the common belief that youth is the best time of life. Many people die young merely because their imaginations will not allow them to accept old-age as a happy, creative time.

Longevity is based upon our expectations. You can add to your life in increments if you focus upon events in the future you wish to enjoy. If people around you contemplate dying shortly after retirement at the age of 65 years, you can instead expect to extend this by five to ten years of happiness and enjoyment. When you reach this age, you can use your imagination and expectation to extend your previous age limitations. It is common in some cultures such as Georgia, Russia to live to 100 years in an active way. This life span follows the expectations of the Russians who expect to live this long.

These long living people never retired from life or stop working. You may wish to retire from your usual employment, but find some vocation or avocation that keeps you creative, vital and involved. In communities where elders live long they are usually actively involved in family and community affairs. Some kind of productive work is essential to remain healthy and to live long.

By uniting physical and spiritual values in our later years, spirituality becomes an integral way of living. Your spirituality will then make your activities hum with spirit and soul. It is essential to have a spiritual life, a personal communion with God/Goddess, nature or whatever you hold most high, if you are to live a long life. This kind of spirituality helps keeps you creative, vital and involved.

Spirituality need not be based upon self-denial and self-punishment in search of self-knowledge. Self love can become an essential part of spirituality. The traditional shadow of the domination by men over women in many religious traditions does not express the highest truth. The more a religion is based upon celebration, equality, love and forgiveness, rather than sin and martyrdom, the higher and truer is its expression. Each of us is a spiritual being in the process of becoming more. We can become conscious magicians if we learn to use our will and love to create our reality.

In creating a spirituality that is rich and active while aging, it is essential that it be based upon active participation. This for me means that I maintain a regular practice of meditation to make a connection with the spiritual forces beyond me that love and support me when I allow it. The core traditional belief of some conservative churches that human beings are inherently bad, sinful or wrong is not only mentally unhealthy, but leads to a shallow, impersonal spirituality. A spirituality that fosters self-love, courage and self-esteem needs to replace ancient religious templates that limit or demean women and all human beings as inherently flawed, sinful creatures.

An antidote to negativity is gratitude. This can be expressed by having fun and enjoying life, especially the richness and beauty of nature. One of my clients, an artist in her mid-seventies, made plans every year to live and work in a creative environment with others artists who could help her grow and produce as an artist.

To live richly, in old age we can continue to seek and grow. We never need to settle and wait to die. If we have fulfilled one life destiny, we can create another which suits our talents and strengths. We can find something we know needs to be done in the world and we are suited to do, and enjoy doing it.

Dying Consciously with Dignity and Peace

In our later years, we do enter the shadow of death, but we do not have to fear that evil will come to us, if we remember that we are eternal, spiritual beings who are on earth to learn and enjoy our experiences for our entire lives. Shamans tell us that when we die, our eight chakra, just over our heads expands and envelopes us in a vessel of light. We are enveloped in the highest part of us, closest to God. We can prepare ourselves for a peaceful death through forgiveness and doing a life review. Family members or healing friends can help us die by allowing us to tell our life stories and granting us permission to die. They can help us by asking, "Is there anyone you need to forgive?" How would you like to be remembered? We can be helped to let go of any feeling of having been wronged or of wronging anyone else. When we are dying, we need to ask for and be given the opportunity to tell each of our close family members how much we love them. This ritual of dying can be a closure of our earthly experience and a process of saying goodbye.

One of the attributes of spiritual adults is their gradual acceptance of their death. Death can be considered as the final metamorphosis in which we again undergo a final change, analogous to the transformation of the larva into a butterfly. Our consciousness in death flies free out of our outworn and often sickly bodies.

In death, we become the butterfly-the imago which we have been growing and transforming ourselves to be. This of course is a great mystery, but also a transformation we have prepared ourselves to take by living more and more from the larger, soul stories of our lives. Our transcendence is always a result of our choosing to live the larger stories of ourselves and achieving the great work we came here to do. I express my feelings toward death best in this poem:

The Landlord of Death

When death comes
to evict me
from the rented rooms of my body
with his dust pan and broom
to sweep me into the ashes of yesterday's fire,
I will change my old, tattered clothing
and step into the dark mansion of mystery.

I will leave behind
what I thought was home
what was only a temporary loan,
the broken bones of change,
the nickels and dimes of dollars
that cannot measure the value
of what there is in me
that will never be lost

> Within all the little deaths and losses
> I have known,
> the white rose opens
> in dreams and reveries
> where I cannot be lost,
> solid ground,
> an island in a turbulent sea,
> a cup held up for me to drink
> containing all the love
> I have ever been given or felt.

In dying, we meet the last face of the soul–that of Soul Return. This face helps us make peace with the life we have lived and forgive ourselves and others. At this time, we can resonate and focus upon connecting with the highest heart energy of unconditional love. Just as good parents place no demands upon a child to earn their love; neither does this divine source demand us to believe in a traditional, orthodox code to earn its love. The divine source loves us unconditionally; it is we who demand conformity to human standards which differ from the divine one.

SHADOW WORK- CHAPTER TEN HEALING
DURING THE LATER-LIFE CRISIS

1   If you have decided to create a new dream or dreams for yourself during the later-life crises, begin to imagine and live it. Ask yourself what kind of life would feel passionate and alive. Take some first steps to achieve this.

2. In meditation, call upon your future self or higher self to talk to you about what may block or impede you from achieving your vision for your future.

3. Take time to write out your old age script using the questions in the text as a guide. What are the beliefs you have about what you expect you will be or do in your elder years. Change the negative beliefs to more healthy ones.

4. Look at the health challenges you have as flags or markers of areas in which you have dark shadow issues. Explore the messages of these illnesses as places you can face your hidden agendas or blockages to heal and grow.

5. How cynical, self-doubting, fearful or pessimistic are you? Use this as an indication of your dark shadow issues. Replace this with positive expectations to achieve better health and happiness.

Reference Notes

Preface
1. Jung, Carl <u>Collected Works</u>: Read, Fordam & Adler: Princeton N.J., Princeton University Press C.S., 14, 1963.

Chapter One-Our Bodies as a Reflection of Our Shadows
1. Duff, Kat <u>The Alchemy of Illness</u> Pantheon Books, a division of Random House, Inc. March 1993.
2. Jung, C.G. <u>Analytical Psycholgy: Its Theory & Practice</u> (Lecture One, The Tavistock Lectures: New York: Random House, Vintage Books) 1968, p.23.
3. Dethlefsen, Thorwald & Dahlke, Rudiger M.D. <u>The Healing Power Of</u> <u>illness.</u> Element Books Limited. Munchen. 1983.(English Translation 1990) P.36-43.
4. Lazaris <u>Working with the Shadow:</u> <u>*An Imperative on the Spiritual Path*</u> Palm Beach, NPN Publishing Inc., 1995.
5. Lazaris The Chakra Tapes, Concept Synergy, Ibid.
6. Limmer, Eleanor <u>The Shadow Knows</u> Freedom Press 2007. p.103-120.
7. Limmer, Eleanor <u>The Body Language of Illness</u> Freedom Press. 3rd Edition, 2004.
8. Pert, Candace <u>Molecules of E</u>motion New York: Scribner, 1997.

Chapter Two-The Body as Soul and Spirit
1. Limmer, Eleanor <u>Balance: Beyond Illness to Health and Wholeness</u>. Freedom Press, 2002.

2. Riso, Don Richard & Hudson, Russ <u>The Wisdom of the Enneagram</u> New York: Bantam Books, 1999.
3. Limmer Poem "Mattering" in <u>An Alchemy of Joy</u>, 2000.
4. Talbot, Michael <u>The Holographic Universe</u> New York: HarperCollins 1991, p. 13-14.

Chapter Three-Healing the Pain beneath Our Illnesses
1. Lazaris Tape on "Ending Pain" Concept Synergy, Ibid.
2. Kabat-Zinn, J. <u>Full Catastrophe Living</u>. New York: Dell Publishing. 1990.
3. Pennebaker, James <u>Opening Up: The Healing Power of Confiding to Others.</u> New York: William Morrow and Co. 1990, P.13-14.

Chapter Four-Discovering and Healing our Collective Dark Shadows
1. Campbell, Joseph <u>Myths to Live By</u> New York: Bantam Books 1973 p. 166-171.
2. von Franz, Marie-Louis "A Matter of Heart" (a film about the life of Carl Jung)
3. Limmer, E. <u>Balance: Beyond Illness to Health and Wholeness.</u> Ibid.
4. Lazaris, "Escaping the Entrapment of Perfectionism' Tape. Concept Synergy. Ibid.
5. Sarno, John M.D. <u>Healing Back Pain</u> New York: Wellness Central, 1991.
6. Lazaris "Healing Hurt" tape Concept Synergy, Ibid.

Chapter Five-The Healing Process
1. Limmer, E. <u>The Body Language of Illness,</u> Ibid. 126-7.
2. Myss, Caroline "Essential Guide for Healers" Sounds True, 2004.
3. Sarno, John. Ibid.

4. Neumann, Eric "The Self lies hidden in the self," in Zweig and Abrams <u>Meeting the Shadow: The Hidden Power of the Dark Side of Human</u> <u>Nature,</u> Ibid. p.6
5. Lazaris, "The Hidden Agendas" Tape, Concept Synergy, Ibid.
   Ibid. "Working with Your Shadow, an Imperative on the Spiritual Path" Tape.

Chapter Six-The Healthy Light Shadow
1. Lazaris, "Harmony, The PowerVortex" Concept Synergy, Ibid.
2. Lao Tau<u>, Tao Te Ching</u> "Thirty" Translated by Jane English, Vintage Books. 1972.
3. Zeig, Connie and Jeremiah Abrams Editors <u>Meeting the Shadow: The Hidden Power of the Dark Side of Human Nature.</u> Los Angeles: Jeremy Tarcher, Inc. 1991, p. 62
4. Kobasa, S. C., S.R. Maddi and S. Kahn. "Hardiness and Health: a Prospective Study," *Journal of Personality and Social Psychology.* 1979. (42) 168-177.

Chapter Seven-Healing of Heart Disease during the Shadow Middle Years
1. Friedman, H.S. <u>The Self-Healing Personality </u>New York: Henry Holt, 1991.
2. Ornish, Dean <u>Love and Survival: The Scientific Basis for the Healing Power of Intimacy,</u> HarperCollins. 1998. p.23-28.
3. Childre, Doc and Martin Howard <u>The HeartMath Solution,</u> p. 213.
3. Limmer, E. poem "The Dark Wood" An Alchemy of Joy, 2000.

4. Seligman, M. Helplessness. San Francisco: Freeman, 1975.
5. Hillman, James The Soul's Code, In Search of Character and Calling Warner Books, 1997. p. 129-154.

Chapter Eight-Healing Cancer
1. LeShan, Lawrence You Can Fight for Your Life New York:Jove Publications, 1977.
2. Kabat-Zinn, Ibid.
3. Temoshok, Lydia and Henry Dreher. The Type-C Connection: The Behavioral Links to Cancer and Your Health. New York: Random House, 1992.
4. Weil, Andrew M.D. Spontaneous Healing, p. 267-277.
5. Lazaris, Ibid. "Escaping the Suffocating Web of Anxiety" Tape
6. Simonton, O. Carl, Stephanie Matthew-Simonton and James Creighton Getting Well Again. New York: J.P. Tarcher, Bantam. 1978.

Chapter Nine-Healing Autoimmune Diseases
1. Roberts, Jane The Way Toward Health Amber-Allen, Inc. 1997.
2. Roberts, Jane Dreams, "Evolution" and Value Fulfillment, Prentice Hall Press. New York, P76.
3. Roberts, Jane Ibid. Volume II. P. 421-5.
4. Conger, John "Jung and Reich: The Body as Shadow" in Zeig and Abrams, Meeting the Shadow Ibid. p.120.
5. Starlanyl, Devin and Copeland, Mary Ellen Fibromyalgia and Chronic Myofascial Pain Syndrome: A Survival Manual, New Harbinger Publications, Inc. 1996, p.315.

6. Lazaris, "Freeing Yourself from the Unspeakable: Jealousy, Envy and Rage" Tapes, Concept Synergy, Ibid.
7. Ibid. "Self-Esteem" Tapes

Chapter Ten-Healing in the Later-Life Crises
1. Jung, Carl, <u>Memories, Dreams and Reflections</u>. New York: Pantheon Books, 1971.
2. Lazaris, Enchanted <u>Wisdom:Windows to the New World</u>. Concept Synergy, Ibid.
3. Limmer. <u>The Body Language of Illness</u>. (on Longevity) Ibid. 125-8.
4. Limmer, Eleanor, poem "The Landlord of Death"

Bibliography

Alexander, F.C. Psychosomatic Medicine:Its Principles and Applications NewYork: W.W. Norton & Company.

Beinfield, Harriet and Korngold, Efrem Between Heaven and Earth Balatine Books, 1991.

Bolen, Jean Shimoda The Tao of Psychology: Synchronicity and the Self New York: Harper and Row. 1979.

Campbell, Joseph The Portable Jung Penquin Books, 1978.

Campbell, Joseph Myths to Live By New York: Bantam Books, 1973.

Childre, Doc and Martin, Howard The HeartMath Solution HarperOne 1999.

Conger, John Jung and Reich: The Body as Shadow Berkley California: North Atlantic Books, 1988.

Dethlefsen, Thorwald and Dalke, Rudiger M.D. The Healing Power of Illness Element Books Limited., Munchen, 1983, (English Translation 1990)

Dossey, Larry Meaning and Medicine Bantam (1981)

Duff, Kate An Alchemy of Illness Pantheon Books 1993

Friedman, H.S. The Self-Healing Personality New York: Henry Holt, 1991.

Friedman, Meyer and Ulmer The Treatment of Type A Personality Alfred Knopf, New York: 1984.

Fritjof, Capra The Tao of Physics Boston: New Science Library, 1985.

Gerber, Richard Vibrational Medicine Sante Fe New Mexico: Bear and Co., 1988.

Goleman D. Emotional Intelligence New York: Bantam Books, 1995.

Hillman, James The Soul's Code: In Search of Character and Calling, New York: Random House, 1996.

Jung, Carl G. Analytical Psychology: Its Theory and Practice New York: Random House-Vintage Books, 1968.

Jung, Carl G. Editors Fordam & Adler Collected Works Princeton N.J. Princeton University Press CW 14, 1963.

Kabat-Zinn J. Full Catastrophic Living New York: Dell Publishing, 1990.

Lazaris Working with the Shadow: An Imperative on the Spiritual Path Palm Beach NPN Publishing Co. 1990. Ibid. Tapes "Self-Esteem" "Escaping the Entrapment of Perfectionism" "Escaping the Suffocating Web of Anxiety" "Chakras" "New Ways of Harnessing and Transforming the Negative Ego" "Healing I, II Tapes"

LeShan, Lawrence You Can Fight for Your Life New York Jove Publishing 1977.

Limmer, Eleanor An Alchemy of Joy Freedom Press, 2000.

Limmer, Eleanor The Body Language of Illness Freedom Press, 3rd Edition 2001.

Limmer, Eleanor The Balance: Beyond Illness to Health and Wholeness: Spokane: Freedom Press 2002.

Limmer, Eleanor The Shadow Knows: How to Understand and Heal its Messages: Freedom Press, 2007.

Mein, Eric Keys to Health: The Promise and Challenge of Holism San Francisco: Harper & Row, 1989.

Moyer, Bill Healing and the Mind "The Chemical Communicators" New York: Doubleday, 1993.

Myss, Caroline Anatomy of the Spirit New York: Harmony Books, 1996.

Ornish, Dean Love and Survival: The Scientific Basis for the Healing Power of Intimacy, Harper Collins, 1998.

Pelletier, Kenneth Holistic Medicine from Stress to Optimum Health Delicorte Press, Seymour Lawrence, 1979.

Pennebaker, James Opening up: The Healing Power of Confiding in Others New York: William Morrow & Co., 1990.

Pert, Candace Molecules of Emotion New York: Scribners, 1997.

Reich, W.Character Analysis New York: Noonday Press (Original work published in 1933)

Reid, T.R. The Healing Of America Penguin Books of the U.S, 2010

Riso, Don Richard and Hudson, Russ The Wisdom of the Enneagram New York: Bantam Books, 1999.

Riso, Don Richard Understanding the Enneagram Boston: Houghton Mifflin, 1990.

Roberts, Jane The Way Toward Health Amber-Allen, 1977.

Sarno, John M.D. Healing Back Pain: the Mind-Body Connection New York: Warner Books, 1991.

Shealy, Norman M.D. and Myss, Caroline M.A. The Creation Of Health: Merging Traditional Medicine with Intuitive Diagnosis Walpole, N.H.: Stillpoint Press, 1988.

Siegel, Bernie Love, Medicine and Miracles New York: Harper & Row, 1983.

Simonton, O. Carl and Matthew-Simonton, Stephanie, and James Creighton Getting Well Again J.P. Tarcher, 1978, New York: Bantam 1980.

Starlangl, Devin and Coopeland, Mary Ellen Fibromayalgia and Chronic Pain Syndrome New Harbinger Publications, Inc. 1996.

Talbot, Michael The Holographic Universe New York: HarperCollins 1991.

Temochok, Lydia and Dreher, Henry The Type C Connection: The Behavior Links to Cancer and Your Health New York: Random House, 1992.

Von Franz, Mari-Louis "A Matter of Heart" Video

Weil, Andrew M.D. <u>Spontaneous Healing</u> Alfred Knopf New York, 1995.

Zukav, Gary <u>The Seat of the Soul</u> New York: Simon and Schuster, 1990.

Zweig, Connie and Abrams, Jeremiah Editors <u>Meeting the Shadow: The Hidden Power of the Dark Side of Human Nature.</u> Los Angeles: Jeremy Tarcher Inc. 1991.

Index